Contents

Foreword

Sometimes, when I am trying to concentrate on a project, out of the corner of my eye, I notice something on my desk related to another project. I start dwelling on this other task, and I get distracted from my work. As Jeff Davidson will explain, it is not the other task that creates the delay but the meandering and lack of focus that steers me away. Lack of organization costs me time and mental energy.

Reading Jeff's newly revised *The 60 Second Organizer* reorganized my mind in preparation for cleaning up my desk. The time I spent reading Jeff's advice prepared my mind for reorganizing in the same way that stretching prepares my body for tennis. This is the way Jeff approaches organizing—as an exercise in control, efficiency, and peace of mind.

When you read this new edition of *The 60 Second Organizer*, you'll learn how each of the sixty tips—one for each minute in an hour—can help you restore order to any area of your life, whether it be your desk, car, or worktable. If one tip can't get you moving, you can easily and quickly flip to one that will. In seconds, you'll pick up a nugget or two and find yourself on the path to reclaiming your life.

Now that my debris is cleared away, I'm beginning to find out more about myself. Maybe I've taken this organization stuff too far . . .

—Warren Farrell, Ph.D., Author,
Why Men Are the Way They Are and
Women Can't Hear What Men Don't Say

2nd Edition

60 SECOND
ORGANIZER

Sixty Solid Techniques for Beating Chaos at Work

JEFF DAVIDSON

BUSINESS

avon, massac

Published by Adams Business
Adams Media, an F+W Publications Company
57 Littlefield Street, Avon, MA 02322. U.S.A.
www.adamsmedia.com

ISBN 10: 1-59869-844-3
ISBN 13: 978-1-59869-844-2

Printed in the United States of America.

J I H G F E D C B A

Library of Congress Cataloging-in-Publication Data
is available from the publisher.

This publication is designed to provide accurate and authoritative information with
regard to the subject matter covered. It is sold with the understanding that the publisher is not engaged in rendering legal, accounting, or other professional advice. If
legal advice or other expert assistance is required, the services of a competent professional person should be sought.
—From a *Declaration of Principles* jointly adopted by a Committee of the
American Bar Association and a Committee of Publishers and Associations

Many of the designations used by manufacturers and sellers to distinguish their
product are claimed as trademarks. Where those designations appear in this book
and Adams Media was aware of a trademark claim, the designations have been
printed with initial capital letters.

This book is available at quantity discounts for bulk purchases.
For information, please call 1-800-289-0963.

Acknowledgments

I have many people to thank for their help in the preparation of this book. Jessica Scism, Jenny Scholl, Cat Hickey, Liz Ward, and Brian Willett helped me in the preparation of this book by making key edits and revisions. Peter Archer, my editor at Adams Media, offered enthusiasm for the revised project and made it a "go," along with Laura Daly, editorial director. My thanks goes to Beth Gissinger in Publicity and Promotions, Phil Sexton in Trade and Special Sales, and Chris Duffy in International Rights and Distribution. My thanks also to Scott Watrous for keeping company operations in the past on an even keel and to Bob Adams for his constant vision and excellence.

Thanks to subject matter experts Michael Gershon, M.D., Barbara Hemphill, Robert Fritz, Nancilee Wydra, Jim Cathcart, Nicholas Lemann, Robert Cooper, Ph.D., Stephen Hawking, Ph.D., Don Aslett, Dr. Wayne Dyer, Robert Levasseur, Jaclyn Kostner, Ph.D., and the late David McClelland, Ph.D., Vilfredo Pareto, and Earl Nightingale.

Introduction

Why should I bother to get organized? Who *cares*? What for? Derek Bok, former president of Harvard University, and not to be confused with Bo Derek, achieved fifteen minutes of fame by saying, "If you think education is costly, try ignorance." If you think getting organized is time-consuming, try disorganization. The increased flow of information and multiplication of data that we're all experiencing has made it imperative that we be better organized and ready to handle the growing volume.

If the places and spaces all around you are always cluttered, what are the potential consequences you might be experiencing? Do you feel overwhelmed by the never-ending lists of responsibilities and tasks that need to be completed? Are you caught up in a seemingly unyielding cycle of work that makes you feel as if you are always running behind? Do you find yourself brushing up against deadlines and sometimes completing projects after they are due? Does thinking about this make you feel as if your head is spinning off in another dimension? If you have answered yes to any of these questions, ta dah! You may have just found the right tool to help you become, and remain, more organized.

Consider the array of situations, places, spaces (both mental and physical), and cyberplaces in your professional and personal life where it probably makes sense to be organized, such as:

- Desks and file cabinets
- Computer files
- Meetings
- E-mail inbox
- Calendars
- Moving to a new location

- Work office
- Paper management
- Accumulations
- Cubicles
- Collections
- Wardrobe

When you start listing everything, the list grows long. You're probably wondering how you are going to tackle each of these areas, while still holding a job and having a life. Fortunately, you only need to understand a few guiding principles and hands-on techniques! And lucky you, all you need to know is in this nifty little volume. We're going to tackle the task of getting organized head on!

Disorganization Is Costly

The negative effects of disorganization may be wreaking havoc on your career, though you may not even realize it. Or maybe you do realize it but can't bear to think about it.

Do you send a negative message to others? Are people reluctant to ask you for help? Are you regarded as someone who is not a team player? Do you end up leaving important tasks unfinished because you are not organized enough to complete them? Are you absent or tardy more than others in your organization? Do you have difficulty finding important documents or files? Do you forget about important meetings and appointments?

Do you have an inability to let go? Does your disorganization represent an attempt to collect and retain pieces of the past? Does this backlog of outdated material hamper your ability to take advantage of current challenges? Does the clutter around you diminish your productivity? Do you feel guilty when you are not engaged in work-related activities? Are you putting in overtime more frequently than you'd prefer? Are you intrigued yet?

These are problems disorganized people know all too well. Beyond the negative effects disorganization may have on your career, also consider what it can do to your personal life. Some people believe that disorganization is associated with anxieties or illness. If you suspect that your health and happiness could be at stake, it's time to face up to the task of getting organized.

Responding to Life

Becoming and staying organized requires effort and thought, while saving time and offering peace of mind . . . okay, a little peace of mind. The not-so-great paradox is that you expend time to save time. If it's helpful, think of getting organized as preparation "to respond to life."

Considering the sea of material goods, constant information, and endless communication that bombards everyone daily, getting organized is undoubtedly a growing problem for you, and you are probably retaining too many items—ones that you have overcollected and overfiled.

No one is born with organizational skills. I've never met a baby who makes to-do lists in gibberish and arranges his toys by color. Everybody has to learn those skills along the way. When you do finally get organized, do you quit after a while, believing it's hopeless to live without the clutter and mess? The key to getting and remaining organized is recognizing how valuable it can be to have everything in order, then making the changes necessary for cutting through the chaos. For many, it is a welcome relief to learn how long it will take. I estimate that for most people, it is the equivalent of about three full weekends and four to five weeknights.

Q: *Say, Jeff, why do some people avoid getting organized even when they lament their disorganization?*

A: Beats me. Maybe they approach getting organized with fear. Some people think imposing order on their lives will take even more time out of their busy schedules, while others are so overwhelmed that they become anxious at just the thought of getting organized. Yet getting and remaining organized is an essential element to a successful career and, possibly, to a happy home life.

How organized are you? If your short answer is "don't ask," have I got a surprise for you: a short quiz. Please use a number-two soft-lead pencil and keep your eyes on your own paper; you'll only be cheating yourself. . . . Now then, if you answer "yes" to any of the following, you've picked up the right book, and this is your time to prevail.

1. Do you spend five minutes or more looking for an e-mail or document? It doesn't take that long to find one simple sheet of paper. Don't kid yourself. If you can't find it, you can't find it, and you certainly can't benefit from it.

2. Are month-old papers on your desk? A desk is not a file cabinet.

3. Do you have trouble finding an item in your desk that you use frequently? Maybe it's best left on top of your desk.

4. Do you feel that you could be organized if you only had more space? More space is seldom the answer; filing, throwing away, or deleting the nonessential is the best solution.

5. Do you have piles of magazines and journals you haven't been able to read? If you're thinking of reading these issues cover to cover, good luck. How about simply extracting the handful of articles that appear most supportive of your efforts on the job or that look most intriguing and letting go of the rest?

6. Did you ever find something at the bottom of a pile that you didn't know was there? Perhaps a file, an old letter, or last Tuesday's lunch? You're liable to lose anything! Condense your piles by eliminating old papers and filing away important ones.

7. Do you have hundreds of e-mails accumulating in your inbox? Why not organize them into files or delete those that are

outdated or unimportant? Handle e-mails as soon as they arrive, then assign them to the appropriate folder or delete them. Never let them build up in your inbox, or just getting a simple message will become a stress!

If none of these quiz questions applied to you, congratulations! You can start with tip #1. If all of these questions applied to you, it still makes sense to start with this tip, too!

PART ONE

Embracing Powerful Perspectives

1 **Lighten Up: Organization Won't Kill You** In the 1950s and throughout the 1960s and 1970s, the Success Motivational Institute, Nightingale-Conant, and a host of other self-improvement businesses emerged. These organizations offered motivational programs designed to help listeners achieve personal goals, including how to get organized.

By the 1980s, dozens of companies had sprung up that offered cassettes, videos, and other materials on virtually all aspects of career and life. These aids ostensibly could help anyone get from point A to point B more efficiently. By the 1990s, such programs were offered via CD and through other digital and electronic formats. Nowadays, you can go online and gather quick self-improvement tips in the time it takes to punch in your credit card number. And what will they think of next?

In the early years, lack of scientific research in the field of human achievement, however, prompted many scholars and journalists to scoff at what the public was being told about self-improvement. Dr. David McClelland of Harvard University was among the most prominent researchers to explore the potential connection between mental functioning and career or personal success. For several decades before his death in 1998, McClelland studied the potential links between what one thinks about and what one achieves.

McClelland was convinced that "men and women of humble origins" could "break ranks" and redesign their lives. Certainly, this is wonderful news for all who ever had a hankering to be all that they could be. Now, here's where you come in.

If you are reading this book, you are probably among those individuals who want to improve life and your career by generating a routine of organization. You have the power to set and achieve your goals of becoming and remaining organized, and to use this power to follow through in other aspects of your life. You have the ability to summon your own personal motivation to overcome the challenges and roadblocks in your path so that you may attain your desired level of organization. So, there go all your excuses. . . .

Here's a new perspective: Getting things in order can be fun, or at least satisfying. If you've ever been to a hockey game and seen the Zamboni machine used between periods, then you've seen a creative approach to a chore. A driver climbs in and carefully circles the ice, laying a thin coat of water, which soon freezes, leaving the rink in brand-new condition—hard, smooth, clean, and ready for the play period. The drivers traditionally make one giant loop around the outermost area of the rink, then come down the middle of the rink, creating two noticeably long semicircles.

In a winding fashion, the driver then completes one-half of the rink, moving closer toward the middle of the half he's currently working on. Then he swings over and completes the other side of the rink. When he's done, the entire floor of ice is smooth, gleaming, and ready for the players. Each organizing task you decide to tackle, no matter how insignificant or mundane, can become a challenging project, like the Zamboni's task. If you have to rearrange shelves, for example, make a game out of rearranging them efficiently. If you have to remove piles that have accumulated around the corners of your office, take it on as a challenge. In many instances, there is no single "right way" to do it, so proceed in a manner that is enjoyable to you. If Mary Poppins can make cleaning the nursery fun, so can you. Just a spoonful of sugar does help the medicine go down—or so they say.

When it comes to getting organized, you have the option of approaching the task in many ways, and you will then be able to successfully monitor your own progress.

2 **Learn Your Organizational ABCs** Ponder this: Why are you able to achieve the things you achieve? The three basic elements to any behavioral change are:

Antecedents
An action or **B**ehavior itself
The **C**onsequences of that action or behavior

These are the ABCs of behavioral change!

Suppose you're driving along a country road on a warm spring day. Suddenly, you see a stop sign. The sign is the antecedent. The behavior derived from this is your stopping the car. As a consequence, you obey the law, avoiding the possibility of either an accident or a ticket resulting from driving through the stop sign. In short, you get to keep on driving! Imagine this same situation, but with a different behavior. You see a stop sign (antecedent), and rather than stopping, your behavior is to ignore it and drive through it. What are the consequences? If no one is around, you might save a couple of seconds and continue on your way. But what if a police officer across the street sees you, stops you, gives you a ticket, and you lose your license? There's a tasty karma sandwich for you. Or, what if you get into a serious accident?

Antecedents precede behaviors, and behaviors precede consequences. When you recall major accomplishments, such as being accepted to college or completing a tough project at work, you discover that these accomplishments follow the pattern of antecedent, behavior, and consequence: A, B, C. Now you understand! Big Bird would be so proud!

When the consequences of your behavior are positive, your experience can be an antecedent for other people. For example, the deadline of the big proposal is set. So you get organized and begin tackling the work weeks in advance. You are well prepared to make the final pitch, and as a consequence, you win over the client. For you, it becomes a piece of cake.

Suppose your coworker realizes how well you've done. The next time he has a similar task, he emulates your behavior and does well. He then gives you a whopper of a Christmas gift at the office party as a display of his gratitude. A, B, C of a different sort.

Virtually every goal you've ever set, and every goal that you will set, is based upon some sort of antecedent. Recognition of opportunity and the fear of pain are the two fundamental antecedents for engaging in behaviors that lead to goal achievement. You proceed in goal-setting behavior based either on opportunity that you envision or pain that you wish to avoid. Pretty basic, right? Pavlov's dog latched on—so can you.

This simple paradigm is complicated by the fact that each person's conception of opportunity for gain is multifaceted. In addition, the ways in which people seek to avoid pain are varied. Some fight back; others hide under the covers. Everybody's different. These two fundamental antecedents are often intertwined in ways you may not realize. For example, your quest to become more organized at work might be for any one of the following opportunity-related reasons. You might wish to:

- Demonstrate competency
- Be recognized as an expert
- Improve your chances for advancement
- Get a pay increase
- Act as a team player
- Use less space at your desk, cubicle, or office
- Set an example in your department

At the same time, however, "avoidance of pain" may be a factor. You may try to:

* Avoid looking like you're swamped
* Comply with your boss's orders and avoid a reprimand
* Not spend so much time searching for misplaced things
* Not appear disorderly to visitors
* Avoid feeling inadequate

Perhaps your motivation stems from your perception that everyone else expects you to maintain an orderly desk, cubicle, or office. Maybe you crave having people regard you as being in control. Or, you want to get organized because you know there is someone out there who is convinced that you can't do it. You'll show him!

When you better understand your motivation for getting organized (the antecedent), you can then take the appropriate action (behavior) that will result in the desired achievement (consequence): A, B, C! It's as easy as 1, 2, 3. The Jackson Five know what I'm talking about.

3 **Mine Your Golden Insights** Consider how *difficult* it is to get started on some projects. Why risk being derailed by a disruption that need not have occurred at all? Regardless of how many times you are interrupted in a typical day or hour, recognize that the interruption itself is not the major culprit. You ask, then, what is? The major culprit is misdirection, dawdling, and downtime on the path returning to where you were and what you were doing. You have to go through the excruciating trauma of starting again. So, my friend, do all you can to prevent interruptions from occurring in the first place.

Hold the phones, bar the door, post a notice, and safeguard your time and efforts whenever you're engaged in organizing a space or place in your career or personal life. You'll finish that much sooner and feel good about what you've accomplished, or at least you'll feel better than if you constantly stop for the little things like answering the telephone, checking e-mail, or trolling MySpace or Facebook for hours on end. A necessary task, I'm sure.

To tap the level of brainwave activity where you can think profoundly, meditate, go for a walk in the woods, or take some other action to vanquish noise and distractions. Some people choose to go on vacation, take a drive, or take a break just by sitting on the break-room sofa. Many people have tremendous moments of insight and resolve while mountain climbing (or so I've been told). Others are able to merely sit in a favorite chair and wait for inspiration to spring forth. Some are able to use commuting time to great effect. The thoughts generated during such times have potentially significant value, but they are useless if not harnessed.

Once you've found a quiet space, literally or figuratively, determining what you want to achieve is largely a question of values. To what type of project are you willing to commit? What areas merit your time and energy? How will you go about accomplishing your goals?

Depending on the nature of your work, your thoughts might be among your most valuable assets in determining where to devote your attention. While many people have recurring thoughts throughout the day, some, if not most of these thoughts go unrecorded. Do you take time to organize your thoughts? Do you remember your ideas, and how to relay them, when they are original and creative? If not, you could be shortchanging yourself in major ways without realizing it.

Organizing your thoughts may have direct applicability to your assigned projects and can only help you. Some may seem amorphous for now, but later, they may take on a more compelling nature. Often, the types of thoughts that get shortchanged (i.e., not recorded) are those directly related to staying organized.

While you can't act on the majority of your innovative thoughts immediately, you can organize them for later action. In a notebook, electronic organizer, on your hard drive, or even on your cell phone, set up a file where you can park the seemingly random thoughts that occur to you throughout the workday. Some people prefer technology, like a BlackBerry or T-Mobile Sidekick, but some prefer a three-ring binder or whiteboard to record notes and later save them to a hard drive. Others might use the traditional calendar planner, jotting down important notes or dates.

Use the back of an envelope or a napkin if that's all that you have to work with at the moment. I don't suggest using the back of your hand or the sleeve of your shirt, but desperate times may call for desperate measures. Then there are those who send reminder e-mails out to a couple dozen of their closest associates, friends, or family, or even to themselves. Scanners, copiers, printers, and other office equipment can be used to record, assemble, and review tasks. Shouldn't you take advantage of these simple ways to organize your busy mind?

Ever since I began using a digital recorder to dictate reminders, and then having the recordings transcribed to my computer, I have seen a world of difference. (See tips #23 and #48 for more information on dictating.)

Suppose you're in a meeting and it suddenly strikes you that buying a certain type of notepad or arranging your desk in a new way could make a dramatic, no, make that a *drastic* improvement in your efficiency. If you don't write down the thought, if you leave it marinating in your busy mind, it tends to overcook and slip away. Ultimately, you never act on the thought, never get to taste the juicy morsel, and you continue to operate in the same ineffective way.

The late Earl Nightingale, a renowned motivational speaker and author, once said, "Ideas are like slippery fish. Unless you write them down, they are going to slip away." The sad reality about novel ideas is that most of those that slip away will not come back. What a bummer! You will not have the same moment of inspiration twice. They are what Professor Stephen Hawking, celebrated astrophysicist and author of *A Brief History of Time*, calls singularities, one-time events. It's up to you to make the most of them.

4 **Ask "Who Created That?"** In his book *The Path of Least Resistance*, author Robert Fritz suggests that you ask yourself a critical question when you're faced with a challenging situation. The question is: Who created that?

More times than you probably care to admit, most of the situations you encounter in your life, and all of those related to staying organized, were created by you. Take your office, for example. Can you name a space, a surface, or even a single drawer for which you are not responsible? Does the wind blow so vigorously through your windows that your papers and files become disorganized? Do gremlins visit each night and mess up everything while you're at home asleep? Usually not.

When you honestly confront an issue, you're bound to concede that you created the disorganization in your work and home. There's no one else to blame. I'm sure you're familiar with a situation that has occurred when coworkers have changed or rearranged things that once had order. At home, certainly, a roommate, spouse, children, or other relatives could have a major hand in the disorganization that you face. In all instances, you, being a person of influence, have considerable control over the level of impact that others have on your organizing efforts.

If you work with "perpetually disorganized" people, you begin to see that your attraction to or tolerance of messy types contributes to the accumulation of organizing tasks. This observation is not meant to convince you to seek a new job, but merely to emphasize that you are the person in control in your life. If work, home, or any other aspect of your life is not organized at a level that is comfortable for you, remember who created or contributed to that situation, and choose to take control.

5 **Choose Wisely** You're sitting in traffic on the interstate highway. It's a sweltering day in August and your car's air conditioner conks out. Do you feel justified in being irritated and cursing not only the air conditioner but the car maker, the car in front of you, and the entire interstate highway system? More positive choices are available.

You could hum a favorite song. You could choose to acknowledge the charmed life you're leading or remember that you've been stuck before, and when reflecting on what happened the last time, recall that the situation proved to be of no real consequence.

You could make friends with the driver of the car next to you, who also looks like he's ready to explode. You could be glad that you live in this country, about what's planned for dinner this evening, or that your children are taking you someplace fun for your birthday. As Dr. Wayne Dyer, bestselling author and psychologist, teaches, how you elect to feel is always your choice. The act of choosing is a simple, but powerful, technique that will aid you in becoming and remaining organized.

By making important choices, you automatically redirect yourself to accept that there is nothing you must do, except maybe pay taxes. Everything else is based on your choice. If you choose to keep working on some task, even one assigned to you, this personal decision is made in the present moment and not based on a prior agenda. The new sense of control over your own life yields a tremendous sense of inner harmony.

What are some of the powerful thinking techniques you can keep in mind as you decide to increase your capacity for becoming and remaining organized? Glad you asked:

- I choose to easily become and remain organized.
- I choose to regard getting organized as a fun and worthwhile activity.
- I choose to easily take control of my spaces.
- I choose to maintain clarity when facing organizing challenges.
- I choose to constantly recognize the areas of life where I'm a master of staying organized.
- I choose to easily learn new methods of becoming organized.
- I choose to associate with people who are highly organized and will serve as role models, mentors, and teachers.
- I choose to approach disorganized situations with calmness and clarity.
- I choose to readily reward myself for my organization victories.
- I choose to feel good about the effort I put forth to get organized.
- I choose to embrace challenging situations methodically and effectively.
- I choose to be an overall master of personal organization.

To reinforce the choices you make, write down or type your choices and post them, or record them and play them back.

How many choices can you make in one sitting? Make a few or many; there is no limit. Choose what feels right for you, and keep choosing. While you're waiting in a bank line, run through your decisions. If you notice yourself wavering, recall the new behavior or feeling that you've chosen. You can choose to overcome rituals that no longer support you, or you can make choices that will help mold you into an expert at organizing your life. Choose to choose!

6 Live and Let Learn A new idea is such a rare thing. We often simply imitate what we hear and read. Nevertheless, you can make choices that are not congruent with your history. If, for example, you have never felt that you had an affinity for becoming and remaining organized, you can make the decision to change that!

In a study published in the 1996 *Annual Review of Psychology*, researchers at Tel Aviv University and the University of Waterloo in Ontario found that "people less able to relate the person of the past to the person they are now may be at greater psychological risk, because they are thinking only in the present and their view of the future may not be developed."

In other words, if you're not able to recognize how you've changed since the past, you're likely to allow your past to unduly influence what you do next. If you walk around the halls of your company thinking, "I've never been good at organizing" and fail to acknowledge how you've changed over the years, or if you can't recall some of your recent organizational triumphs, you're needlessly putting yourself down. Reward yourself for the organizational challenges you have overcome! Don't be such a Debbie Downer!

Getting stuck in the past is a major problem for entire nations as well as individuals. "Many international conflicts have their roots in divergent interpretations of the past," say the researchers. (Think about how much time is still devoted to arguing about the Civil War, which ended seven score and four years ago!) So your problem may spring from the fact that people frequently react to the present as if they were still living in the past.

For many of us, "The past represents the context in which people acquire knowledge about future possibilities." Too many people formulate their forecasts from what they recall of the past and what they perceive in the present. Therefore, it behooves you to draw accurately upon your past and note what's different about today. You live, you learn. Alanis Morissette has been saying it for years. Only then can you make clear and confident choices about what you want in the future.

Did you get all that? So, you want to be more organized? It's within your power! Rather than living life looking through a rearview mirror, go where you've never gone before to set and reach goals that might have once seemed beyond your ability. Perhaps the power to achieve them was within you all along.

7 **"Work Smarter" More of the Time** You've probably been advised before to "work smarter, not harder." This sage wisdom is routinely dispensed to people who need to become and remain organized. Or to those people who study ten hours for a fifteen-minute quiz, which doesn't make any more sense than continuing to live a disorganized life. If you had precise information, a team of knowledgeable advisors, and an abundance of relevant resources, I suppose you'd have the opportunity to "work smarter, not harder." But what does "work smarter" actually mean in the real world?

Was Thomas Edison working smarter when he tried and failed to identify a suitable filament more than 8,000 times before creating a commercially viable light bulb? After he finally found the right filament, did his IQ suddenly rise? Working longer and being open to new ideas can lead to working smarter. With hard work, you can learn about your subject and develop more efficient techniques, but hard work is not synonymous with long hours. Perhaps the term "focused work" or "intense work" is more appropriate.

Simply telling someone to work smarter is not enough. If merely telling someone to do something were enough, supervising people would be a breeze! I believe that the true message behind the adage "work smarter, not harder" is that we all need to take a little time to reflect on what we want to accomplish. Perhaps you can work smarter by striving to be a little more organized each day. Then you can start heading in a positive direction and assemble the requisite resources to finish a project. You increase the odds that you'll be able to accomplish the job more quickly and easily.

A profound way to "work smarter" is to follow your inner wisdom. It's inside of you somewhere! There is far more to your instincts, intuition, or gut feelings than you might think. Scientists in the field of neurocardiology have discovered a "brain in the heart." Comprised of more than 40,000 neurons of various types, along with a complex network of neurotransmitters, proteins, and support cells, it acts independently of the head. "This heart brain," says Robert Cooper, Ph.D., "is as large as many key areas of the thinking brain and sufficiently sophisticated to rate as a brain in its own right." And no, this isn't science fiction!

Heartbeats aren't merely mechanical pumping pulses. They have an intelligent language that influences how we perceive and react to the world. There really is a language of love! Each and every heartbeat is linked to the thinking brain and affects both branches of the autonomic nervous system, continually influencing our perceptions and awareness. Cooper says, "The heart is not only open to new possibilities, it actively scans for them, ever seeking new, intuitive understanding."

But wait, there's more! Pioneering research by physiologists and gastroenterologists indicates that there is also another "brain" inside the intestines (hmmm . . .). Known as the "enteric nervous system," it is independent of and interconnected with the brain in the cranium, according to Michael Gershon, M.D., who occupies the chair of Anatomy and Cell Biology at Columbia University. There are a lot of people who only think with their enteric brain instead of their cranial brain, and most of them are on reality TV.

Cooper observes that "gut instincts are real and warrant listening to." And he literally means your gut! For most of the organizing challenges you will face, you probably have a strong idea as to how to best proceed. Often, you don't follow your own inner wisdom. You let yourself be pressured by external sources that, in retrospect, offer little contribution. Next time you feel something in your stomach, it might not just be your lunch talking, so listen up!

The solution: Rely on your instincts more routinely. In other words, use all three of your brains! Decisions based on instincts and intuition rapidly and automatically encompass all of your life experiences and acquired knowledge. If you're figuring out how to organize something, it's often okay to simply start and let your intuition guide you. Every aspect of your being goes into making a decision based on instinct or intuition. Your decision isn't whimsical, random, or foolish. Trust your brains; have you ever known your intestines to be foolish?

8 **Proceed with Pareto's Principle** Vilfredo, Vilfredo! In 1897, Italian economist Vilfredo Pareto discovered a key relationship between effort and result now known as the Pareto Principle or the 80/20 rule. He found that 80 percent of what someone achieves is derived from 20 percent of the time that individual expends. Results, outputs, or rewards tend to come from a small proportion of the inputs or efforts directed toward achieving them. Specifically, 20 percent of your organizing efforts will yield 80 percent of your desired effect. Imagine that—one-fifth of what you do accounts for four-fifths of what you accomplish! Success suddenly doesn't seem so difficult to manage after all.

Unhappily, most people devote 80 percent of their efforts, which only yields 20 percent of their returns! Macro effort, micro result—know the feeling? The key to effectiveness is to identify the 20 percent of your activities that are most important, those that yield the greatest results. For example, straightening the pens on your desk may be satisfying, but it likely doesn't improve the quality of your work. On the other hand, carefully adding new information into your contact management software could be the lifeblood of your business or career, and it will get you a whole lot further than having a color-coordinated Post-it collection ever could. Sometimes doing less pays off.

When the Pareto Principle was specifically applied to business, startling observations followed. Within an insurance agency, for example, 20 percent of the agents were found to produce approximately 80 percent of the sales. In a hardware store, 20 percent of the floor space accounted for 80 percent of the profits. In an accounting firm, 20 percent of the clients generated 80 percent of the revenues. It made sense for such firms to find lucrative, long-term clients, to focus their energy and attention on the most profitable percentage, and have the strength to let go of the weaker clientele.

Sometimes you've got to trim the herd to help nature along. Similarly, it makes sense for you to focus the precious time you have for organizing in those areas where it will do you the most good. Your needs will differ from others even in your own company or family. A logical way to streamline your efforts is to concentrate on those areas where breakdowns are all too frequent. These problem areas are easy to spot. They're signified by time wasted, lost opportunities, accidents, and other negative indicators. In others words, give up pretending that dealing in minutiae will generate large rewards. Finally, a legitimate reason not to sweat the small stuff.

9 **Get in the Mood** When you wait until you are "in the mood" to get organized, you run the risk that the right mood will come at an inopportune time or even not at all! Consider the professional writer who steadfastly maintains a writing quota of a certain number of words per day. The writer who vows to complete 1,800 words by noon each day will complete 9,000 words in a typical work week, and 36,000 words in four weeks. Whether or not the writer "feels like it," the daily writing quota ensures the achievement of a desired output. I mean, this book didn't just write itself, you know.

You may argue that forcing yourself to meet a word count serves little purpose if the writing isn't good. However, writers who set such quotas tend to self-correct as they proceed. Therefore, the words written on any given day are roughly as effective, coherent, and on the mark as the words written randomly on any other day. Occasionally, the daily performance level dips a bit, but this is offset by other days when the performance level exceeds expectations.

Similarly, you may accomplish the most when you are "in the mood" to organize, but it is important to focus on your efforts even when you are feeling rather unenthusiastic. When it comes to getting organized the mood might not strike often on its own. Sometimes you have to force yourself to be in the mood.

Getting organized requires less motivation than being a professional writer. You can set your daily quota of organizing tasks at a low level and still achieve good results. By doing something—regardless of your mood—you're further ahead than if you did nothing. You may not manage to complete a task on your first attempt. However, it's to your benefit to at least try to start.

Peering from the peak of one mountain, the next mountain doesn't look so far. When you're down in the valley, though, hiking and cursing through a dark, entangling rhododendron thicket with a dull machete, reaching the next peak can seem extremely difficult even if you're already more than halfway to the top. So when you're making your way through a cluttered file cabinet, it may seem as if your task is insurmountable. Yet, with only a tiny bit of effort, you can make more progress than if you hadn't tried at all.

Stop believing that you have to "feel like getting organized" and instead, proceed based upon your desire for results, such as tidying the top drawer of your desk.

10 **Give Yourself a Round of Applause** If keeping things organized doesn't come easy for you, use basic psychology to increase the probability that you'll achieve one success after another: Reward yourself. You could be an expert in this area.

Some people who are reasonably adept at rewarding others for a job well done, however, are often curiously deficient when it comes to rewarding themselves. If you have staff members, you may pride yourself in giving them positive reinforcement when they have demonstrated good behavior. How often, however, do you practice positive reinforcement with yourself? You deserve ten more minutes of break time, too! Start rewarding yourself for all the hard work you've done! With the right treat, even the oldest dog can learn a new trick or two!

The key to making your system of self-rewards work is to:

- Make the reward commensurate with the effort (i.e., you don't buy yourself a Mazda for straightening up your desk).
- Give yourself the reward soon after your accomplishment. If you finish cleaning the yard, there is little psychological connection to any reward you give yourself three weeks later.
- Form a solid connection in your mind between your effort and the reward, and then use that as motivation to get started on whatever else needs to be organized. Some people find it helpful to identify the reward in advance.

If you decide to tackle that file cabinet you've been ignoring, and you know that after your magnificent triumph you're going to treat yourself to a new pair of shoes, you can form a clear image of the reward as you proceed. This helps particularly if you feel your energy lagging or you begin to lose sight of your goal. Some individuals, including me, prefer to determine the reward spontaneously. Once I've "aced" some organizing task, I walk around my office or home with the mini-mission of stumbling into something I enjoy doing. It could be picking up a favorite magazine, visiting a favorite Web site, having a snack, or even taking a snooze.

A sparse word to those prone to gluttony: Be cautious that the majority of your rewards for jobs well done are not related to food. It's too easy to slip into the trap of continually rewarding yourself with some sweet, yummy snack. Even if you employ healthful snacks, such as carrot sticks, an apple, or a rice cake, you still run the risk of equating accomplishment with food consumption.

I'm not saying to rule out food as one of your rewards; simply make it one of an array of potential rewards. After all, rewarding yourself with a cookie for working out today seems a little counterproductive.

Master the mini-reward: If your organizing project is sizable and/or long-term in nature, divide your task into segments, with planned mini-rewards along the way to keep you going.

Suppose you're reorganizing your office, a task you've dreaded for the last eighteen months or however long since there was last a clear path to your desk. Your conservative estimate is that the project will take at least three hours. Nine small, self-generated rewards at twenty-minute intervals might help you persevere in what otherwise might seem to be an entirely arduous task. Surely you can make it through twenty minutes.

As you proceed, sometimes you get into a rhythm or a flow and have no need to stop after twenty minutes. That's fine; simply pause when pausing feels right and appropriately reward yourself. Your ability to positively reinforce your behavior at periodic junctures as you proceed is vital.

Maybe you're the type of person who wants to break only after an hour, or you prefer to have only one break in the middle. For some tasks, I know I won't be satisfied until I have completed the whole darn thing and that if I pause, I will lose impetus. In such cases, I regard completion of the entire project as a reward in itself, and when done, I have no problem at all taking a run, watching a favorite show, going to a movie, dedicating a monument to myself, or figuring out some other type of reward.

Sometimes you're making great progress on a huge project when, despite your best efforts, your energy starts to wane. You can employ a variety of self-generated rewards to keep going and give yourself periodic breaks and other critical time-outs. Nevertheless, you will encounter some tasks that you just can't bear to continue to tackle that day or at least for the time being. Here, it is critical to know when to stop.

Many books will tell you how to get started and how to keep in motion once you have gotten started. Knowing when to stop can be as important as anything else on your path to becoming and remaining organized.

If you're mentally or physically exhausted, and you induce yourself to proceed past some optimal point, you may actually diminish your willingness and ability to pick up on the project again later that day, or the next day, or whenever you had intended to resume working on it. Especially for larger organizing projects, knowing when to stop can be one of the most subtle, key components in pursuit of your desired end result. Who knew that not organizing would be so important to getting organized!

What are some of the telltale signs that you have hit the wall and it is best not to proceed any further for now? Here are just a few:

- After having taken several breaks and giving yourself appropriate rewards, you find yourself simply going through the motions and not making any real progress.
- You start making costly errors.
- Your productivity drops off.
- You have completely lost track of your mission.
- Staying on the project any longer would jeopardize your ability to give your attention to other important tasks and responsibilities.
- You are missing a critical resource and while it is admirable to attempt to make do, no further significant progress is expected.

- You become so disagreeable (in the case of working with others), it makes sense to reconvene later today, tomorrow, or at some other scheduled time.
- You fall asleep mid-task.

Finally, if you can't remember what you're working on, give yourself a break!

PART TWO

Enveloping Provocative Practices

11 **Stop Making Excuses** Even when you know it makes sense to begin a task, too many excuses keep you from getting started. Here are eight wimpy ones for not getting your hands dirty:

1. "I have been meaning to . . ." If this sounds familiar, then make getting completely organized a high-ranking item in your life. See tip #18.
2. "I have never been good at organizing." No worries, mate. All is forgiven. Those "not good" at organizing believe that somehow things "simply get out of order," "get lost," or just up and walk away of their own accord. The difference between people who are "good at organizing" and those who are "not good" is that organized people recognize the effort required to maintain order.
3. "I don't know how to get started." Keep reading.
4. "I have so many other things to do." Of course you do; you will for the rest of your life. After getting organized, however, the other things you "have to do" will more directly support your priorities and goals, and you will have a clearer image of the connection between your work and your achievements. Read tip #19 and reap the benefits.
5. "Organizing will take too much time." For most people, it takes three weekends and several weeknights. Okay, maybe you need longer than that! Go back and reread the introduction and keep considering what disorganization has cost you.
6. "I don't see any value in organizing." Although you may not realize it, many aspects of your life are already organized. Now you are about to enhance personal control, which has great value, by extending the procedures you may already be using.

7. "It makes me anxious; I don't feel that I am accomplishing that much." If you only toss unnecessary papers or delete unnecessary files and e-mails, creating more space, you will be accomplishing a great deal. Imagine what all that freed-up memory will do for your computer's speed!
8. "My dog ate my BlackBerry." Don't laugh. Some people will say anything to avoid organizing their messy lives!

When you're able to forsake excuses about getting organized, you open yourself up to some worthwhile achievements. Thereafter, getting organized emerges as a regular and vital preliminary step to the things you want to accomplish.

12 **Practice Being Imperfect** At times, striving for perfection is appropriate: A medical doctor performing a complex operation, a pilot landing a plane, and a police detective investigating a murder all strive to do the best possible job. When your brain is on the line, it's okay to expect perfection from your surgeon. Yet, even for people in these professions, there are situations where perfectionism is unnecessary, unwarranted, and overly time-consuming.

For the doctor, a bandaging job after an operation, regardless of how neat it is, should stop bleeding. For the airline pilot, a landing where one wheel touches down a half second after the other will not diminish the quality of the flight. For the police detective, not interviewing an eleventh witness after interviewing ten witnesses who independently corroborate one another's observations will probably be okay.

Studies show that the additional time you spend to take a project from the 95 percent mark to the 100 percent mark is, in most cases, not worth it. If only I knew that years ago! Striving for perfection—that is, ensuring that the final 5 percent is correctly done—often takes as much time as the initial 95 percent of effort required!

When giving instructions to your staff, if you give them nine or ten suggestions on how to effectively do a job but forget one or two suggestions, they will still have plenty to work with. Conversely, if you strive to give them every great suggestion you can offer, the time and effort that you expend may be unnecessary, and the marginal value of the extra suggestions for your staff may not be worth the effort.

In your own work, there are countless instances throughout the day when not being "perfect" makes more sense from a practical standpoint than striving for perfection. If you're turning in a report, and your department is structured so that the production team does the copyediting, it doesn't pay for you to slave over the project trying to produce a 100 percent grammatically and tactically correct report. When you assemble data to make a decision, if you wait until you have reams of information, the opportunity in question may pass by and be lost. What's more, if you collect too much data, you can become more confused than informed. Practice makes perfect, but sometimes perfect can make you crazy!

Many decisions, as we've discussed, can be made based on instinct and intuition and still turn out fine. When you make a decision, although you may not realize it, you're actually drawing upon all of the information to which you have ever been exposed. Let go of the quest to overcollect. Intuition works in many cases, although there are some situations—like considering a potential spouse—where you'll want to know a few more things.

Hereafter, assemble the body of information necessary to help you feel comfortable with your decision, but do no more than that. Likewise, look for other opportunities throughout the workday when a 90 to 95 percent effort will be fine.

13 **Begin Easily** Have you ever fallen into this trap? You accumulate a pile of stuff that is begging to be organized, but you have trouble tackling the task because you tend to over-complicate things. Maybe you have a streak of perfectionism that prompts you to believe that the task is going to take more time than is necessary to get comfortably organized. Perhaps you seek to arrange items in the most judicious order possible and like Adrian Monk, you have to arrange, then rearrange, then rearrange everything all over again.

If any of the above types of thinking plague your ability to get organized, banish them to the far, far corners of your mind and accept this general principle:

Sometimes the best type of organization is the simplest.

Consider an everyday example. Your desk is a disaster. You've looked at it day after day, and eventually you can't tell where the mess ends and the desk begins. You dread the thought of having to put everything in order. You may even be secretly hoping that a tornado will come tearing through your office today and carry everything away so that you don't have to face the mess. Yet, deep down, you know that it will be to your extreme advantage to get your desk in order. Even an F5 tornado sweeping through wouldn't make you feel any better about your desk—if you still had one, that is. Why not allow yourself a simple start, thereby decreasing the pressure on yourself and increasing the probability of your success?

A quick first step would be to round up all the pens and pencils that populate your desk. Put them in a pencil holder, can, or container.

Next, grab all the Post-it pads, note pads, and scraps of paper that contain any vital information, be it an address, a phone number, or a Web site.

Then, decide here and now to do the following:

1. Enter the information on your hard drive or electronic planner in a folder that is designed to be a catchall for such tidbits of information.
2. Lay down these Post-it pads and scraps of information on the copier to create one or two collective pages to be neatly filed or folded and parked in the corner of your desk for quick reference. (Clue: If you have all such tidbits in one place, you have a better chance of finding and using them as needed.) Ideally, you don't let such tidbits pile up to begin with; however, if this is a habit, you are probably going to keep doing this without even realizing it.

Now, collect all the file folders on your desk. These files represent tasks or projects that you'll be tackling. Make sure each folder includes the appropriate materials, then refile all the files except for those that you will be working with this morning or this afternoon.

Next, gather up any books, reports, or other large documents, and place them on the appropriate shelves.

If you need specific pages from such documents, copy them on a copier, put those pages in the corresponding file folder, and put away the original books, documents, and reports. Better yet, move to a more paperless system and use the office's electronic files or scan hardcopies to create PDF files that can be neatly and easily stored on your computer's hard drive. That way you can save your sanity and a few trees while you're at it.

By now you're probably well on your way to becoming more organized. Clearing your desk is not that big of a deal. Make it simple. Tackle similar items such as pens and pencils all at once, then go on to the next type of item, and the next, until the desk is back under your control. You can do it. You will even live to tell about it.

14 **Make Hay by Using Your Milestones** Attention future high school and college graduates: When you finish school, it's understandable that career-oriented goals will begin to predominate. Will you get a job? Will it be a good job? Will it be at a decent salary? Will you have to relocate? Will Mom and Dad let you move back in because you're afraid to launch into the "real" world? Will you forget everything you've ever learned? You probably embarked upon a course of study that prepared you for a specific line of work. Many people, however, haven't done this.

When it comes to your career aspirations, the best time to get organized is before you graduate from school—a significant milestone. The more time you give yourself to plan careers or lifetime goals, the better your chances are of success.

If you start getting organized the day after you graduate, you may find yourself underemployed, underpaid, and undervalued. You may even find yourself unemployed and living on a friend's futon. The graduation milestone is sufficiently noteworthy for most people to prepare for what they want to do afterward. You can harness that same sense of clarity and feeling of unity as other milestones come into range.

Everyone has milestones in his or her life. Do any of these ring a bell for you?

- Your new job
- Marriage
- Buying a house and relocating
- Having children

- Selecting a day-care facility
- Going back to school
- Saving for your children's education
- Traveling
- Caring for your parents
- Retiring
- Coping with health problems

You can employ these milestones as aids in your quest to become organized. Pretend you're approaching your fortieth birthday. (This might be frightening for you to imagine. I myself am dumbfounded by how long ago that was.) What sort of physical shape do you want to be in? In your office, what files are not worth retaining? What files need to be created?

You turn forty only once. Milestones and events need not be of the once-per-lifetime variety. There are recurring events throughout the year, within particular seasons, and in the course of a month, that can serve as useful markers. On your quest to become more organized, your assignment is to recognize the value and practicality of acknowledging a wide variety of approaching milestones and events. Hereafter, use them as rallying points to spur your efforts. Let's look at two such milestones.

Relocating
With all of humankind's scientific, medical, and technological breakthroughs, you'd expect that someone would do something about the onerous task of relocating! Most people change residences after college graduation, marriage, an increase in income, and so on. Yet, there doesn't seem to be any way around loading and unloading every single thing you own, item by item, box by box, into a car or truck. You can hire people, but the process of

moving is no less upsetting. There are change-of-address cards to mail, phone numbers to change, bills to reconcile, utility companies to call, not to mention new nosey neighbors to deal with.

Moving does demand a high level of organization, at least at the outset of, and directly following, the move. You have to decide whether particular items will be transported, sold, or given away. You're forced to make decisions you wouldn't otherwise have to make.

Beyond the physical move itself, there's something about the moving process that facilitates order. If you're married or living with a significant other, a move can be a wonderful time to mutually reorganize your possessions and living space. ("We're not keeping that ratty old couch!") Perhaps you agree to let your partner have more space in the new location, or you both agree to set up a home gym. This is the opportunity to decide exactly how you want to arrange your new home.

I had a friend in college who landed a job with Amtrak in Washington, DC. During my friend's youth, his father worked for a *Fortune* 500 manufacturer and was frequently relocating to assume new positions. Because the family moved every couple of years, they made decisions regarding which items to retain and which to toss. In the new location, they frequently lived in a clutter-free, streamlined home. When his family settled down for the long haul in a southern Connecticut suburb, even after many years passed, they still maintained an organized, clutter-free household. This family might seem too perfect to actually exist, like the six Brady Bunch kids sharing one bathroom, but I'm positive they weren't figments of my imagination.

The notion of organized living appealed to me long before I became a conference and convention speaker on the topic of having more "breathing space" and less clutter in your life. My friend's home was a pleasure to visit, unlike others' houses that were strewn with stuff in every room. I'm not saying you have to move frequently to maintain a clutter-free home. However, it certainly helps. The next time you move, recognize that a new opportunity to organize your space comes with it.

Likewise when you move from one office space to another, you have the marvelous opportunity to set up your new workspace free of all that stuff that cluttered up your old space but really didn't add to your productivity or peace of mind. So, look upon any interoffice moves as a chance to come clean!

Organizing Before and After a Job Change

Relocation can occur in life without actually moving from one place to another. Seeking a new job may be the start of an occupational relocation. Starting a job, whether or not you are currently employed, represents a variety of challenges. As emotionally nerve-racking and mentally draining looking for a job can be, it's one of the fundamental opportunities you'll have in life to get organized. When else do you have clear, uninterrupted stretches of time for determining exactly what's important in your life and career?

Perhaps you got fired or left your previous job under less than pleasant circumstances. Maybe you're new in the workplace and have never had a career position. You may be re-entering the career world after many years. In any case, you're where you are for a reason and you have a marvelous opportunity to set your sights on what is most appropriate, challenging, and enjoyable for you. Clarity can help you get a job that is more consistent and more aligned with what you want to do in life and where you want to be at your age.

You may encounter other career milestones that naturally and spontaneously prompt you to reorganize. These include a large pay increase, your appointment to a special/high office, or your election as an officer in your professional association or group. A non-career-related milestone could include being asked to serve on a special committee supporting your town council.

When any of these kinds of events occur, given the new situation, you may find it fitting and appropriate to re-examine your office, your files, or your life. Hereafter, whether you are moving to a new location, a new place of employment, or a new stage in your life, take advantage of those opportunities and reorganize.

15 **Endure the Worst First** If you fail to file your taxes on time, send out birthday or greeting cards too late, shop for presents at the last minute, or struggle with desk drawers that are jam-packed with garbage, then it is in your best interest to change the way you handle such tasks. Any time you have control over the sequence in which you tackle responsibilities, handle the seemingly unpleasant elements first. As author Brian Tracy would say, "Eat that frog." If you save what you like to do for last, and handle the unpleasant things such as administrative tasks first, you maintain order a bit longer.

It sounds so easy, but why do people resort to old, unproductive ways of approaching their day? Bad habits or routine behavior have far more of an impact on daily activities than we might imagine. Research shows that the more an individual engages in a particular behavior, the stronger the neural pathways in that person's brain become, which encourages them to continue the behavior. What all this means to you is, if you allow piles to build up in your work area, as time marches on, you will keep on creating the clutter.

If you're involved in the same exercise regime, or lack thereof, chances are you will continue on that same path. Alarmingly (at least to me!), research shows that if you continue living by these habits long enough, your ability to change literally decreases.

As you get older, decades of habitual behavior, habitual thought patterns, and a habitual life all but ensure that your capacity for change in the years to come will be a fraction of what it might have been ten, twenty, and thirty years ago. This does not mean you can't change. Chances are, however, that you will need extraordinary motivation, such as your boss telling you to straighten up your desk or else!

It is an axiom of life that if you're seeking to develop a new habit, the best possible time to begin is now. The false promise of beginning something next week or next month is a disguised form of procrastination. The energy and anxiety that you invest in putting off an activity can consume more energy than required to perform the activity. Contemplating a change does have value, but germination has more value. So often the changes that you are resisting require less effort, energy, and time than you think.

The longer it's been since you attempted to get organized, the more likely you are to encounter steep challenges. If procrastination is your enemy, then action is your friend. Remember the findings of Mr. Newton—a body in motion tends to stay in motion. As such, the tiniest action toward getting organized can start you on a winning path. It's definitely preferable to taking no action at all. A small action could consist of clearing your desk, making a purchase, finding a helper, visiting a key Web site, or prioritizing tasks, or in Newton's case, sitting beneath a tree and getting hit on the head by an apple.

16 **Take the Plunge for Sixty Seconds** One of the most effective techniques you can use, true to the title of this book, is to engage in organizing activities for one minute at a time.

Suppose your office at work is a federally declared disaster area. You don't want to begin turning things around. Actually, you dread the task. Promise yourself that you will engage in an organizing activity for a single minute. You can set a timer, look at the clock on the wall, or sing the alphabet song three or four times—whatever works for you.

For sixty seconds, straighten up whatever you can. In the course of a minute, maybe you can only tackle one area. Conceivably, you can handle two or three items. Put away or discard extraneous items and neaten up any portion of your desk that will contribute to your overall quest.

Bzzzzzzz. At the end of sixty seconds, honoring your promise to yourself, stop and return to whatever you were doing previously.

Depending on the time of day, when the spirit moves you again later that morning or afternoon, return to your one-minute routine. For sixty seconds, organize some part of your office. As unpalatable as the task may be, by engaging in it for only sixty seconds, you'll make some progress and feel better about yourself.

As with other techniques presented throughout this book, you'll find that after sixty seconds, you often don't want to stop. The momentum of your efforts carries on to the next minute and the next. As this happens, be supportive of yourself. Let yourself "go with the flow." Believe me, you'll stop when you want to, have to, or are too tired to proceed. Still, it's amazing how much one minute's worth of straightening up can do for most of the places and spaces in your life.

I've seen people clear out and reorganize a desk drawer in a minute or so. I have observed others who rescue their desktops from overflow in sixty seconds or less. I've witnessed others clear away shelf space or simply make a path through their offices

during these sixty-second campaigns. You can even read and finish the shorter tips in this book! You'll never know how much you
can accomplish during this time until you try. So try it; you might
like it! What's more, you'll experience a world of difference.

17 **Ponder the Question, "Will It Be Any Easier Later?"**
When you find yourself facing a pile that needs to be organized, ask yourself a key question: "Will it be any easier to handle
later?" Will organizing the pile somehow miraculously be less of a
task in the future than it is right now? If the chore will be signifi-
cantly easier at some point in the foreseeable future, then you may
remain in a state of relative disorganization, secure in the knowledge
that you will put things in order later. If only that were always true.

About 99 times out of 100, however, the best time to tackle an
organization task is right now! Later, the mess before you is likely
to be worse. Piles grow higher. Files grow thicker. Stuff accumu-
lates! Have you noticed?

By asking yourself if it will be easier to handle the task later,
you automatically create a personal incentive to deal with it now,
independent of what your mood happens to be. Whether it's disas-
sembling the pile, reducing the size of the file, organizing an overflowing inbox, tackling the car glove compartment, or managing
other spaces or places, getting organized is nearly always an easier
task if you get started sooner. And let's face it: you're not getting
any younger, either.

What if asking, "Will it be any easier later?" does not serve as a
great prompt to initiate your organizing task? Perhaps you have a
problem with procrastination, not with organizing. As such, you'll
be well served by my companion book *The 60 Second Self-Starter*
(Adams Media, 2008), which offers sixty tips on overcoming procrastination. Many of them will give you that "kick-in-the-pants"

start that you need and probably want—although not literally, as that would be unpleasant and leave a bruise.

Identify What's Thwarting You

If you find yourself completely unable to get started on a task, it may be because a legitimate obstacle or a temporary roadblock hampers you. Your excuse may actually be, drum roll . . . valid. The task may well prove to be easier later! It happens. Perhaps the organizing task is too big for you to handle alone and you need help. Maybe you don't have the right tools or equipment. Perhaps you lack the budget or monetary resources realistically required to do the job. Maybe this is not a good time to start due to weather conditions or environmental factors. (This excuse does not, however, work when you're organizing your office, so don't even go there.)

What if a forthcoming event renders your efforts temporarily futile? Suppose you desperately want to clean and reorganize your car. It's become so disorganized you want to howl in the night. Tomorrow, however, you're taking a key buyer and his assistant to lunch. They're probably going to track some dirt and particles in and out of the car. Still, you don't want to risk having them see the inside of your car as it usually is. So you clean it.

Now suppose you're taking your daughter and two of her friends to the state fair. They're going to accumulate banners, posters, stickers, and stuffed toys. Someone is bound to spill a drink or crush an oily French fry deep into your carpet. You are likely to find popcorn pieces and cotton candy trapped in the crevices of your seats. Are you visualizing this?

Would it make more sense to clean and organize your car now, or the day after taking a group of kids to the state fair? You guessed it (you're so good!). Postponing your organizing efforts for a day or two in this case is a better use of your time and tends to yield greater peace of mind. Who wants to whip the interior of the car into shape only to have it spoiled a day later, necessitating further efforts? Not me!

Do the kids actually care if they ride in a clean car or not? Like, well, do they even, like, notice? For this and similar situations, you're better off waiting until after the event and then proceeding with your organizational plan. And after that mess, I'm sure you'll be wanting to clean before your car becomes some kind of health hazard.

Identify what's thwarting your efforts at getting organized. If a more appropriate start time emerges, yield to it!

18 **Organize According to Your Priorities** Living a clutter-filled life requires no particular skill—anyone can get the hang of it. Who is the most likely to be unorganized? It's those who haven't identified their priorities and established supporting goals.

To organize effectively, it helps if you identify your priorities. Otherwise, you're organizing without a goal. Priorities are broad elements of life. They are so basic that you can often misplace them somewhere in your go-go schedule. Start identifying your priorities, and you'll realize that much of the clutter you have collected does not serve you or support what you have deemed to be of importance. Much of what you've assembled in the places and spaces of your life is useless! Harsh, I know, but so true!

The five-step procedure that follows is simple and direct and will help you to establish priorities.

1. Write down everything that is important to you, assigned to you, or that you seek to achieve. Feel free to make this list long and involved.

2. Several hours later or even the next day, revisit your list. Cross out those things that, on second reading, are not that crucial. Combine any items that appear similar to each other. The object of this second encounter is to dramatically pare down your list. If you have too many priorities, you are likely to feel anxious and frustrated. We can't all be Superman.

3. Now, restructure, redefine, and rewrite your list if necessary; seek to streamline it. When in doubt, toss it out. If you're unsure if an item belongs on the list, chances are, it doesn't.

4. Put your list away and take it out the next day or the day after that. Now review it as if you are seeing it for the first time. Can any items be combined? Can anything be dropped? Should anything be reworded? As always, if something seems as if it is not that important, it probably isn't, so feel free to drop it!

5. Go ahead and make a working list of what you feel are your priorities at this time. Yes, things will shift and change as time marches on, but this is your list for now.

If it's helpful, use variations of the following phrasing in composing your choices:

- "Achieve financial independence"
- "Strengthen my relationship with my boss"
- "Provide for the education of my children"

By wording your priorities in this way, with an action expressed by a verb, you are more inclined to take action than by simply jotting down "happy job situation," or "children's education," or "money, money, money."

As months and years pass, your priorities may shift. That's understandable. Since they are based on what you identify as important in your work and life, as changes occur in your work and life, it makes sense that your priorities might change as well. For now, concentrate on the important areas in your life that you have identified.

Be sure to print your priorities on a small card that you can keep in your appointment book or wallet, type into your electronic day planner, or even glue to your forehead; whatever it takes for you to keep track of your priorities. This affords you the opportunity to review your priorities periodically throughout the day, particularly when you are stuck in a line somewhere. It is too easy to lose sight of the things we have deemed important in our rush-rush fast-paced world. Simply reading your list of priorities on a regular basis is a powerful and reinforcing "self-organizing" technique.

Who says you can't move "get organized" or its counterparts such as "maintain clarity" or "stay focused" to the top of your list? Such a quest may not even be on your list at the moment. In the short term, however, it may make great sense to assign getting organized as a high priority, particularly if you ever want to find that priority list again. Getting organized as an interim priority will help you to pay homage to your other longer-term priorities.

Amaze Yourself

When you actually commit to get organized, you sometimes astonish yourself by how much you can accomplish in a relatively short amount of time. What if you were to spend one day, one morning, or merely the next (solid) hour putting things in order? What if you treated the activity as if it had vital importance in your career or personal life? If you deemed getting organized to be of great importance, then, like other important things in your life, you would tend to it.

If it helps, get your priorities in order with organizational software for your PDA. A program like PlanPlus, by Franklin Covey, lets you prioritize tasks, set goals, capture information, and stay organized. You can scout for others on *www.shopping.yahoo.com*, *www.google.com/products*, and the other huge search engines.

The way things are unfolding these days all but dictates that getting organized is one of the high priorities in your life, even if heretofore you haven't recognized it. As a basic point, you need to be organized for reasons of safety. In nearly any environment, if things on the floor or items are out of place, you can trip over them, bump into them, and find yourself in a hazardous situation. Don't let your coworkers find you starving, bleeding from thousands of paper cuts, with crushed ribs after days underneath a two-ton pile of out-of-control papers.

Especially in the workplace, being organized translates into finding items more quickly and easily, being more responsive to others, and being more professional. Such characteristics contribute to the progression of your career and to your potential to receive raises and promotions. If you doubt this, recall the messiest person in your workplace . . .

- Someone who routinely loses things
- Someone whose office is not a pleasure to visit
- Someone who is unreliable in returning borrowed items
- Someone who resembles Charlie Brown's friend Pigpen

Have you got that person in mind?

How likely is that unorganized individual to be picked for a team when team members have the option of choosing? How likely is that person to receive a raise or promotion when there are others who are doing equally well and remain organized as they do their job? Is this person you? You can see where this is heading! All things being equal, actively using and demonstrating organizational skills is one of the ever-present, if unarticulated, methods you can use to enhance your overall career prospects. Viewed in this light, it's relatively easy to make getting and staying organized a higher priority.

19 **Etch Your Goals in All but Stone** Now comes the part where you take action in support of those elements of your life you decided are important! Establish a variety of goal statements that correspond to each of the priority areas you have chosen. Seek to present these statements in positive terms, using positive terminology. If one of your priority areas is career success, and you have been the office clutter-bug for ten years, it will not help to set a goal such as, "I will not clutter my desk for one week."

What happens during that week? You begin to dwell on avoiding clutter day after day, hour after hour, until you become ineffective in doing your job. A more effective goal statement would be, "I will maintain a clear, clean desk this week." You can only master the organizational walk of life with baby steps. I think I can, I think I can . . .

Any goal worth pursuing will need to be:

- Written
- Quantified
- Assigned a deadline

Writing your goals positively helps solidify your efforts. There is something about having your goals in a place where you can review them that makes them more real. There's no way to ignore them when they're right in front of you! At a minimum, a visual reminder is a confirmation of their importance. At the most, they represent a formula guiding you to highly desirable end results.

"Quantified" means you attach a number. Say you want to receive an increase in salary of $4,000. The request is $4,000, not $3,975. If you happen to exceed your goal—well, lucky you!

A "deadline" means that you choose a specific target date (and time for goals of short duration) to complete what you set out to do. "The middle of the week" is vague. "Wednesday at 4:00 P.M." is specific. If you want to meet your deadlines, be specific!

Identifying priorities and establishing goals in support of those priorities is relatively simple compared to what comes next. Anybody can establish goals. Unfortunately, most people's goals are forgotten days or weeks after they first establish them. Consider the going success rate of New Year's resolutions. How many people actually lose those ten pounds? Reinforcing the goals that you set so that you actually achieve them requires something more than merely plans or words. Namely, it requires action!

Fortunately, there are many techniques that you can employ to see that you stick to the goals you set for yourself.

Uniting with others, particularly with those who have goals in common with you, is a time-honored tradition. For example, someone who wishes to have more peace of mind at work might join a meditation group on weekends. Someone seeking to stay fit and look the part of a rising executive might seek a running partner. Those who want to enhance their erudite knowledge by reading great books might seek to join or start a book club. Uniting with others could mean simply finding a team member who wants to achieve the same thing you do at the same time you do.

There is something about engaging in an activity with others that helps to ensure progress will continue. You feel accountable.

When you have no one to share the activity with, it is easy to slide. When someone is trying to achieve the same result as you, it's easier to have the support and encouragement from the coworker, colleague, friend, spouse, or whomever, than to have no one there to keep you motivated.

Suppose you tell me that you are going to accomplish XYZ by next week. Then when we meet next week and I ask you about your goal, you'll either tell me that you accomplished it, or you'll tell me that you are somewhere close to achieving it, working on it, or haven't done anything about your goal at all. Simply knowing that we will be meeting and discussing your progress could be the driving force that you need to be successful in accomplishing XYZ.

Visualize the completion of your goals; it's another powerful technique for increasing your probability of success. Many top athletes today visualize successfully completing the foul shot, catching the touchdown pass, hitting the home run, completing the triple axel jump, or clearing the hurdle, before actually doing so. By visualizing their performance, they increase the odds of a successful performance. Likewise, virtuoso pianists, ballet dancers, and professional speakers visualize successfully engaging in the task at hand before actually performing. If it works for them, surely it can work for you.

You can visualize successfully organizing your office, desk, or any aspect of your work or life, and thereby increase the probability of succeeding. You probably visualize all the time, thinking about how it is going to be when you are with a loved one, having dinner that evening, or on vacation next spring. You can use the same process to see yourself becoming more organized at work. So put those daydreams to good use.

Any goal, large or small, lends itself to the visualization process. Simply find a quiet place where you won't be disturbed, close your eyes, and let your imagination take hold. See yourself accomplishing exactly what you want to accomplish, in the way you want to accomplish it. See yourself as organized, in control, relaxed, and ready in ways that you know you can be.

Surround yourself with reminders that you will constantly be exposed to. Using sticky pads or small notes, write out goal-reinforcing statements and post them on your mirror and in your appointment book, on the dashboard of your car, on or near your nightstand, on the refrigerator, in the refrigerator, by your front door, and wherever else you are likely to pass during the course of a day. Pleasantly surprise yourself! Type them into your PC or palmtop, and record yourself reading them.

Devise something that is uplifting and supportive of your efforts like, "Today is going to be a great day for organizing my file cabinet." Vary the statements so that you don't start to ignore them. Add smiley faces, or rainbows, or stars if you insist! Put them in creative places where you know you will encounter them and where they will have the most impact.

I like to leave a note to myself in my appointment book at the end of each day. Then, when I open up the appointment book to start the upcoming day, I see the uplifting note, routinely give myself a broad smile, and start working!

20 **Lay Claim to Your Goals** To reorder their lives on a grand scale, some people devise an elaborate set of goals. It is the nature of a plan, however, not its complexity, that most affects its success. You are truly on the path to getting organized if your goal is a conscious and healthy one, a self-initiated choice. When you lay claim to a goal, make the goal yours, you don't need out-side stimulators. When you're willing to take responsibility for the outcome, a goal indeed belongs to you. A wonderful gauge for determining whether or not you truly are committed to your goal is to think about how you would feel if the goal were taken from you—something of a King Solomon approach. Suppose you could no longer proceed down your chosen path, and all activity in pursuit of your goal had to cease.

- Would you be outraged?
- Would you object?
- Would you fight for your right to continue?
- Would you seek to avenge your goal to the death?

If you didn't achieve the goal, and you never laid claim to it, you could easily walk away from the task with no regrets. If you laid claim to a goal and didn't achieve it, you would have lingering feelings that you had failed yourself.

If a goal is not originally your creation, perhaps you have some leeway in the situations you encounter and can engage in shaping the goal. You may have to complete the entire store inventory, for example, by the end of the month. There are plenty of things you can do to make the task more enjoyable and rewarding for you, ultimately making it your own goal. Perhaps you can tackle the job one aisle at a time. Or, you may choose to begin with all of the high-priced items. By approaching an externally imposed task as a challenge, such as getting organized, it can be seen in a different light and internalized as your own goal.

When your mother used to tell you to clean your room, you probably did so grudgingly, since you didn't adopt the goal as your own. Hers was an edict that you "had to," although you disliked it. Sure, you were pleased with the results and would even have agreed that the room looked better and was more functional in an organized state. How much easier, however, would it have been all those times if you had adopted the goal of cleaning and organizing your room as if the goal were your own? It might have saved you a lot of misery from all the kicking and screaming in protest.

Today, the same solution at work potentially prevails. If you have been given the task of organizing financial records or the meeting room, before getting started, take a few moments to contemplate the task:

- What will be involved?
- What kind of energy will you lend to the assignment?
- What will you do first?
- How will you take charge?
- How will you feel when the task is completed?
- Is it really worth throwing a temper tantrum over?

Can you personalize this task—make it your own? Of course you can! Even if it's a serial task to which you've been assigned, personalizing it makes it easier. You'll find that your attitude changes once you've made the goal your own.

- Straighten the literature rack in the reception area? You bet, and when it's done, it's going to be the premier literature rack in the whole office complex.
- Clean up that filthy workbench with its layers of dust, loose bolts and screws, and rusty old tools that you've had forever? Picture yourself as the guy or gal who receives the admiration of everyone for the tool collection mounted on the shop wall.

PART THREE

Listing and Charting Your Way

21 **Become Your Own Management Tool** An organization management pitfall, particularly in recent years, is to rely on sophisticated scheduling tools as if they were the be-all and end-all. It makes sense to use palmtop organizers, electronic calendars, time management software, day planners, and so on, if such tools:

- Support the way you live and work
- Are simple and convenient for you to use
- Are easy for you to keep current

A $100 bill says that you can't name a management tool that won't let you down the minute you don't keep the information it holds up to date. Recognize that all tools you use to manage your time, from simple to-do lists to complicated scheduling software, require continual input and updates. Otherwise, they quickly fail to reflect the current tasks and responsibilities you face. Even with voice recognition management and static or online scheduling tools and the ability to access the Internet through cell phones and PDAs, you still have to "feed" the system.

With any planning or scheduling tool, someone has to be in the driver's seat. If you're not keeping up with the timelines you have established, particularly if you are relying on a scheduler in coordination with others, it will quickly become ineffectual. Likewise, if you bite off more than you can chew, planning and scheduling tools may alert you to what you have done, but it is up to you to get back on track and not rely on them too heavily. In that respect, the most critical factor in organizing, planning, and scheduling at all times is you! Ah, but you sensed that all along, didn't you?

Until sophisticated organization management tools come packed with a mechanical arm that literally moves the items accumulating on your desk, logs them in using a barcode system of some sort, and then ranks them based on your current task list and schedule, such tools will depend upon you, not vice versa. If you let them down, they will most certainly let you down. Until management mechanisms check your IM, e-mail, fax machine, and voice mail, and assess and rank what each of those messages represent in terms of what you have to accomplish in the next hour, day, and week, halfheartedly using even sophisticated technology will only put you out of sync.

Said most simply, your brain remains the most important tool in organizing your schedule, your time, and your life. The mental energy you bring to maintaining your organizing system is what fuels your efforts. Get some rest. A clear mind is a fundamental step on the path to a clear desk and an organized life.

22 **Schedule Time to Organize** Did you ever stop to think that you can schedule some organizing tasks in your appointment book, palmtop scheduler, or online calendar much as you would any other important obligation? If your desk is a disaster area that even FEMA couldn't make worse, if you don't know what's in your overflowing drawers, and if you find yourself spending untold minutes throughout the day hunting for crucial items, why not schedule some organizing time for later today or tomorrow?

Scheduling organizing time? Gimme a break. Won't that represent another burden in a long line of tasks you face? Not so! Scheduling organizing time increases the probability that you will actually engage in essential organizing activities. It also reduces guilt. Many people feel as if maintenance tasks, such as getting organized and staying organized, intrude upon all the other "important" things scheduled in their day. If you fall into this camp, then you take your cue from others who have found that formally scheduling sessions for organizing automatically raises the task to the status of an important commitment. Think of it like a date instead of another work appointment—a hot date with some organizing aids, and you don't even have to buy them dinner.

The mere fact that you have scheduled a session on your calendar gives the task of organizing the proper weight and a sense of importance that the task would not otherwise accrue. When Tuesday at 2:30 arrives, for example, and it's time for you to organize your second file drawer, you dutifully find yourself attending to the task much as you would any other item scheduled for that day. If you allot forty-five minutes, then give your full attention to the task for that entire block of time, and at the end of the forty-five-minute session you're not finished, you'll at least be much further along than if you had never scheduled such a session!

Go ahead and schedule time to organize your computer desktop and files. The time you devote to such a task could prove to be satisfying and rewarding beyond what you might currently imagine. Here's a bit of organizing wisdom to ensure that you can efficiently use your equipment. How often have you slugged your way through a new software program without bothering to read even the summary card of instructions? You learn enough to be proficient, but you never master the program. You're willing to undertake trial-and-error approaches to getting things done. Sometimes you get lucky and things work on the first couple go-rounds. Bolstered by a few successes here and there, trial and error becomes your standard routine. Too often, however, you spend endless amounts of time going down wrong paths, experiencing more errors for your trials, and still you have no intention or even notion of actually reading the directions.

You need to stop and take the time to devise a system—which initially makes for slow going, but ultimately pays off in terms of increased time savings with each deployment. Many of the systems that we could devise to make us more productive and to help us avoid throwing our time at a problem simply require taking an organized or more methodical approach to learning. For example, we could choose to name our files in methodical ways so that they are more easily recalled and found. We could create a system for selecting and remembering passwords more easily so that we wouldn't be stuck each time we have to enter a password. For example, you could pick the state in which you were born and insert a progression of numbers in the middle, for example, Ore-222gon, Ore333gon, and so on.

When it comes time to learning new software on my computer, I want to spend zero seconds fiddling with instructions and spend the bulk of my time getting things done. So I schedule time with college students who know computers and the Internet like the backs of their hands.

Item by item, function by function, we review both what I ought to be able to do with the equipment and what kinds of things I want to get done as a result of being able to use the equipment. Then, we codify everything into a system. We list the steps, item by item.

After my gurus depart, I have the sacred set of instructions. Now and then, yes, I still run astray. No problem, I'll park that one for now, and at the next possible opportunity my gurus make whatever modifications are necessary to the instructions. By and by, we hone and refine any set of instructions that require modifications. No endless bouts with the instruction manual for me.

The larger your organization, the greater the chance there is someone with whom you can strike up a business relationship. They help you with all things technical and you help them with some skill you can teach which they wish to master. Or you pay them! Whatever works.

So, systematically you name your files, devise and save instructions, and back up your sacred disk! You have the wherewithal to store files on a second, perhaps portable hard drive, a DVD, a USB key drive, or whatever floats your boat.

If scheduling sessions simply to get organized or having a PC/Web guru assist you sounds pointless, humor me and go along with the suggestion anyway. Schedule such a session on your calendar right now, and as the day and time approaches, give it your full attention and full resources, as you would any other item deemed worthy of appearing on your schedule. You may be pleased, if not outright surprised, by the result.

Put New Life into Deadlines

Harnessing the power of deadlines in your schedule can also aid you in accomplishing objectives. Up until now, you may have dreaded deadlines and regarded them as restrictions imposed upon you that routinely foster stress and anxiety. However, deadlines can serve as powerful motivators toward the accomplishment of your goals. It all depends on the way you look at things!

I have written thirty-six books, and another eighteen revised editions, but I wouldn't have finished book one if I tried to "write an entire book." Rather, my goal in approaching each book is to write one chapter at a time. Since most chapters are made of two or three subsections, I simply aim to finish one subsection, then another, then another until I finish a whole chapter. The rest of the day seems like a vacation.

The next day, I go back and start another chapter, approaching one subsection at a time. All the while, I acknowledge that I have a contract to honor and that a publisher is breathlessly waiting for my material. We pick a date in advance, and I agree to turn in the manuscript no later than that day.

Realistically, what do you think the chances are that I would turn in a manuscript on time if the publisher said over the phone, "Oh, we would like to have it in by 2014 or so"? The odds are that I would finish sometime after the twenty-first century. Having a contract that says "on this date, the author will deliver the entire manuscript" dramatically increases the probability that I will finish the book in a timely fashion. Thus, I will be able to get it into your desperately awaiting hands as soon as possible.

What deadlines do you face? Although your deadlines are probably imposed by external sources, you can turn them around with your newfound insight and use them to your advantage. (Hint: One of your deadlines comes around every April 15. That's your favorite one, I'm sure.) What deadlines can you impose upon yourself to increase the probability of completing organizing goals that you have established in support of your priorities?

23 **Balance Today's Tasks Versus Tomorrow's** Everyone I know in the work world uses some kind of list as an organizing tool for getting things done. I'm neither for nor against any particular system you might use to stay efficient. Judge any system by your own personal results. However, if you haven't considered using what I call the super-long to-do list, give it a try.

If you already maintain some type of to-do list, you can use it more effectively to support your priorities by strategically lengthening it without overloading yourself. Your first super-long list will probably fill two to five pages. You'll have a clear idea of what you face all on one big roster, and you'll keep your priorities sharp for years to come. It doesn't have to follow a completely logical order at first; as you'll see momentarily, you can easily move items up to the front as needed. The front page contains tasks to accomplish in the short term.

The dilemma you're most likely to face is balancing the short-term against long-term tasks and activities. I have maintained a ten-page to-do list for years. I had hundreds of things on my to-do list, arranged according to my major life priorities. To keep from going crazy, I make sure most of the tasks on the list are medium- to long-range activities, and these do not appear on the first page.

In essence, I maintain a dynamic to-do list; it contains everything I want to get done, but always with only one page I need to look at: the top page. The first page of my list represents only the short-term activities—those I have chosen to do immediately or within a week. I draw continually from the ten-page list, moving items to the top as it becomes desirable or necessary to tackle them.

Yes, I am forever updating the list and printing out new versions, but there are so many advantages that I wouldn't think of doing it any other way, and you can't talk me out of it. You can keep your list digital if you're not a fan of hard copies. Also this affords you even more mobility and ease, as you can take your file with you on your iPod or electronic planner or even portable storage drive. I review the entire list periodically, always moving items from later pages up to the front page. Thus, anxiety stays at a low level.

Maintaining a long to-do list has helped me become more proficient in managing long-term or repeated tasks. Consider a situation where you have projects due, people waiting for your results, meetings to attend, and so forth. If I am working on a long-term project, I will continually draw to the front those portions that can be handled in the short term. Likewise, if a task is a repeat or cyclical project—something I have to do every month or every year—I can move it up to the front page at the appropriate time without burdening myself by trying to constantly remind myself, "Oh yeah, in four and a half months I need to call that guy again and set up an appointment."

Most people who maintain some type of to-do list and tend to it on a daily basis allow their lists to carry over to the next day. Whatever they didn't finish on one day becomes part of the next day's to-do list. That's okay, but seek to finish today's tasks today.

Don't fall back into the procrastination trap just because you might think you can get away with it. Besides, think of all the ink you'll save if you don't constantly have to rewrite the same lists over and over again.

Certain tasks, such as those that involve recurring organizational efforts, often receive short shrift when it comes to to-do lists. Don't shortchange yourself when listing recurring tasks. They deserve your attention, too.

In the hubbub of each day's activities, you might add certain stellar tasks to your to-do list, such as:

- Organize the magazine rack
- Clear off the desktop
- Rearrange the supply cabinet

Such chores probably don't make your to-do list because they may not be vital, glamorous, or even remembered. Of course, when disorganization reaches a critical point and begins to cost you in time, energy, or effort, it becomes an emergency. If a work or a leisure area gets so messy that you can't use it, the clutter begs for attention. Listing organizing tasks on your to-do list before the situation develops into a mini-crisis helps you to stay in a "preventative" mode. This works well in other aspects of your life, so why wouldn't it work well here? For example, if you take your car in for a tune-up before you suspect a problem, you often spend far less money than if you had brought in your car after it had broken down. And you feel a lot better after taking your car for a "checkup" than you do after spending two hours walking to a gas station and then another two hours trying to find a tow truck in the middle of nowhere at 2:00 A.M. (It was a bad night. Don't ask.)

Likewise, if you do things to maintain your health on a regular basis instead of waiting until you need a quadruple coronary bypass, you tend to live a longer, healthier life. Too many people short-change their health until after they've had a life- or health-threatening wake-up call. When it comes to the continuing challenge of staying organized, listing specific tasks on your to-do list will help you develop a "preventative maintenance" approach that will keep many organizing tasks from ever becoming large and unwieldy, and in the case of your kitchen, smelly and unpalatable. Yuck.

On occasion, you can end-run the to-do list and accomplish tasks without even entering them on your list. Most people who encounter information worth retaining and make a note of it, find that it may stay there for days, maybe months. To deal with incoming data faster, remember that useful information usually involves calling or writing to someone else.

Here's a way to skip several steps, cut down on the clutter, and increase your effectiveness on the job. Rather than adding a new task to your to-do list, try a fast-action option:

Pick up a pocket dictator, cell phone, or any recording device and immediately dictate a letter or memo to whomever you need to contact about what it is you've come across, or dictate or type a message on your computer for immediate transmission by fax, e-mail, or instant message. Voice recognition software is getting so good that in a matter of minutes you can be talking into a microphone as your computer enters your words on the screen. Say it and send it is becoming a one-step function.

How many times a day do you add to your to-do list when you could simply dictate a letter or memo or type or talk a message onto your computer screen and cut your overall time and effort by 75 percent?

24 **Create a Clarifying Checklist** Checklists are wonderful, and, I'll be darned, you are already a master at producing checklists! "Not me," you say? Well, what do you think a to-do list is? It's a crude checklist, often hastily composed with the items listed in no particular order. Even your grocery list is a checklist in training. When it comes to getting organized, a few enhancements to the familiar to-do list will serve you well.

A checklist can have fewer than three items or more than nine items, but for practical purposes, a list usually works best within these limits. Too short and you don't exactly have a checklist. Too long and the list becomes overwhelming; you look at the list and think, "I'll never complete all this."

Pick one organizing task that needs immediate attention. To the best of your ability, create a to-do list (a checklist) of three to nine steps that will ensure your success of completing that one task. What will you need to do first? What will you have to do second?

As you compose your list, be gentle on yourself. The important issue is to first establish a plan. If you haven't worded it correctly or established the most logical sequence, do not fret.

Review and refine your list. Change the order of some tasks, combine some, elaborate upon or divide up others. Ultimately, you will devise a sequence that represents a workable checklist, or you will devise a moronic sequence that leads to your doom.

When would you change the order of items on your list? When the spirit moves you! No need to delve into heavy analysis. Your on-the-fly rearrangement is usually based on ultraquick, unconscious internal calculations as to what should go where and why! Trust your internal wisdom and re-read tip #7.

Now, assuming your effort leads to workability and not doom, honor your efforts by completing the checklist items as you listed them. Tackle the first task first and take it all the way to completion. The list itself might just be a work of art, but it is not meant to frame on the wall. If you can't proceed to completion, take it as far as you can, then go to task two, and so on.

Suppose your challenge is to reclaim control of your department's resource library. Here's what your checklist might look like:

1. Clear the entire room.
2. Dust the center table.
3. Dust and clean the shelves.
4. Evaluate the documents taken from the shelves.
5. Chuck what is outdated, reshelve what is relevant.
6. Invite someone to witness the results of your efforts! (In case you think no one will ever believe that you did it!)

When you receive praise for your efforts, the positive reinforcement increases the probability that you will extend your organizational efforts to other places at work and away from work.

Maintain a Project List

You may be facing several organizing tasks in and around your office and car, and within your desk, briefcase, wallet, or purse. Rather than attempting to tackle them all semi-concurrently, focus on one area at a time. If it helps, make one major clarifying list that cites each place or space that you want to organize. On the other hand, you may not have enough paper or disk space (hee-hee) for the number of lists you'll need. . . .

The list could be ranked based on order of importance, estimated number of hours to completion, or degree of difficulty.

Periodically review the list and pick the organizing tasks you've listed that you have the physical, mental, and emotional strength to initiate. Once you begin on the selected task, strive fervently for completion—proceed all the way to the end of what it takes for you to be fully organized in this area.

Alternatively, if the task is large or multifaceted, such as re-arranging your four-drawer file cabinet at work, sifting through hundreds of saved files on your hard drive, combine your efforts with the advice from tips #10, Give Yourself a Round of Applause, and #60, Divide, Literally, and Conquer.

Keep the list in a handy place, where you can find it easily and peruse it often, whether it is a physical Post-it on your desk or an electronic Post-it on your PC desktop. Having the list handy is more important than you might think. Today, many items compete for our time and attention it's easy to lose sight of what we want to accomplish. Everything gets churned up in the daily grind of having too much to do. The simple act of preparing a clarifying list of organizing projects and periodically examining the list can help you enormously.

25 **Map Your Way** For some people, preparing an outline of what needs to be done is drudgery, whereas a visual plotting, sometimes called a mind map, is less onerous and, dare I say it, even fun. If you're a visually oriented person, you may find relief in mapping out your organizational quest. It's like a treasure hunt! Take any particular organizing task that you face and, to the best of your ability, describe the task in a brief, simple phrase. Write that phrase in the center of a piece of paper and circle it. Taking you back to your middle-school days, isn't it?

Then, from the circle outward, draw a line with an arrow at the end of it to the first thing that comes to mind.

For example, if you are a newbie employee seeking to become more knowledgeable about your company's top customers, and thus far you haven't done squat, the organizing task that you write in the middle of your page might be "Research the top customers." The first line with an arrow might point to a second phrase such as, "List the five top customers."

From there, you might have options as to how to gather data, what sources to tap, and how to store what you find, each of which could merit its own arrow. If it helps, write the name of each information source at the end of an arrow. Returning to your central task (in the middle of the page), contemplate your first move in organizing your "Become more knowledgeable about top customers" campaign. Another line extending from your central task might read, "Obtain online materials." Since your company may already have a customer database, you might not have to spend much time or energy getting started.

As a corollary to consulting the company database, or Web-surfing for information, you might also want to acquire the respective customers' hard-copy brochures, literature, and catalogs. In any case, additional lines with additional arrows should point to these adjacent tasks.

Some people find it helpful to use colored pens or highlighters to stimulate creativity and make the page more visually pleasing. The key is to let the "sparks fly" as you create your visual map. You don't have to answer to anyone in the process. If you want to use boxes, little squares, stars, or any other symbol, it's up to you. If you want to connect tasks by broken lines, dotted lines, double lines, or squiggly lines, you're in charge!

Soon your page will start to fill. Beginning in the center and branching out in many different directions, you create a visual map of the key activities and tasks involved in organizing and executing your "know the customers" campaign. Likewise, you could use a single sheet of paper to map out other organizational challenges. When your map is complete, or mostly done, start using it as your trail guide. Execute the tasks as you plotted them on the special page. (Also see tip #27, "Plot Your Path.")

26 **Chart Your Course** BlackBerries, Sidekicks, iPhones and cell phones, as is widely known, enable you to take your plans with you as you travel, maintain your database of contacts, send faxes, keep up with e-mail, and log on to the Internet to listen to your favorite tunes from anywhere in the world. With the accelerating pace of new technology, you can become a walking, talking organizational wizard and get by nicely without a little help from your friends. Several varieties of organizing and planning software are on the market, and enable you to:

- Organize your daily, weekly, and monthly schedules
- Align your daily activities with important and urgent tasks
- Engage in project planning
- Participate in virtual meetings
- Share files
- Electronically link your plans and schedules with others

The underlying components of effectively organizing your day while making progress on selected tasks and projects remain the same. Any goal that you intend to achieve needs to be written down, quantified, and assigned a specific time frame. If you don't have a timeline attached to a task or project, then "any time" will do, and "never" is the likely result. Never, by the way, is a long time.

More powerful, feature-laden scheduling software, calendar systems, and other project organizers become available with each passing month. Most of these support tools offer some highly convenient common elements, including the following:

- A calendar system for keeping and tracking appointments, identifying schedule conflicts, and flagging areas and times of critical activity
- A variety of chart forms, including milestone charts, flow charts, and calendars
- Touch screens, with drop-down menus, drag-and-drop techniques, and convenient icons
- The flexibility to add or subtract activities in any sequence
- Colors, symbols, and other tools that offer at-a-glance viewing
- Alarms and monitors that toggle on and off, set at times and intervals at your whim
- The ability to e-mail or download any file
- The ability to download music, video, documents, and myriad other resources
- The ability to track stock options and balance your budget
- Multiple options for printing any chart
- Access to phone numbers and the Internet

No matter how sophisticated the technology you may be employing, it will be of little use if the information you are adding is not current or is inaccurate (see tip #21). The geeks have been right all along—garbage in yields garbage out. With scheduling and organizing tools, nothing in yields nothing out! Even your iPhone will be of no use if you don't know how to access and update your information. Still, it does look pretty snazzy.

Whether you use more sophisticated project management and scheduling software on your computer or electronic organizer or cell phone, or you use nontechnical types of tools, such as hand-drawn charts or grids, carefully plotting your steps will lead to these highly desirable results:

- Significant increase in your probability of accomplishment
- Greater productivity
- Effective time management
- Less stress and heartache

The three basic forms of project management and/or scheduling tools are milestone charts, flow charts, and calendars. These tools are briefly discussed in the following tips.

27 **Plot Your Path** A milestone chart, formally known as a Gantt chart, after originator Henry L. Gantt, is probably familiar to you. Depicted here, it offers you a quick view of your progress on a variety of tasks and projects in relation to time:

	Month 1	Month 2	Month 3	Month 4	Month 5
Task 1	»»»»»»»»»»»»»»»»»»»»»»				
Task 2	»»»»»»»»»»»»»»»»»»»»»»»»»»»»»»				
Task 3			»»»»»»»»»»»»»»»»»»»»		
Task 4				»»»»»»»»»»»»»»»	

Here is how it works: Suppose one of your priorities is to advance in your career. One of your goals in support of that priority is to achieve a raise of $6,324 at the next quarterly performance and appraisal session, scheduled in eleven weeks. To reach that goal, you've identified five tasks that will greatly enhance the value of your services to your boss and the higher-ups in your division.

These tasks include:

- Rewriting the orientation manual for new hires
- Getting an article published in one of the top three magazines in your industry
- Starting an online monthly newsletter for your firm's top clients and prospects
- Completing the report three weeks before it is due
- Participating at the key trade show by making important contacts, and gathering critical information for your boss

Adding these five accomplishments to your performance record over the next eleven weeks, along with what you already do in the normal course of the day and week, will be challenging; but hey, they don't call you Wonder Woman for nothing! Your mission now becomes to allocate your time and resources to complete each of the tasks with a flourish and to position yourself for the salary increase you're after.

A more sophisticated visual tool is to plot each of the activities on the milestone chart so that you have a clear indication of both the timeline and sequencing of each of these activities, and how they will support your overall goal.

To begin, plot the most basic information for each project. Then, extending the process a bit further, add subtasks under each task area. For example, to get the article published, you may first have to interview some people or conduct some research. These could be depicted as subtasks. You might have to organize your notes, create an outline, then write a first draft, then possibly a second draft, and have a colleague review the article before you submit a final draft. Finally, you will be able to submit a final draft to publishers.

Task	Item										
	1	2	3	4	5	6	7	8	9	10	11
Rewrite manual	»»»»»»»»»»										
Publish article		»»»»			»»»		»»				
Online zine				»»»»»»»»»»»»»»»»»»							
DEF report					»»»»»»»						
Trade show							»»»				

28 **Introduce Subtasks to Your Chart** Depending on how much detail you need or can stand, you may have anywhere from six to ten subtasks in support of a given task. How much detail you choose to portray in the chart is your choice. The important thing is that what you record is of value to you—it helps you continue your progress toward your chosen goals. With the other tasks, you may find yourself plotting anywhere from two or three subtasks to fifteen or more.

Continuing with the example of arranging to get an article published, you would want to list the level of detail that serves you. If you complicate the chart, it could be counterproductive to your purposes. To enhance your chart, add symbols such as a broken line, which can denote germination, or put footnotes at the bottom; place left and right arrows, which can indicate distinct periods of activity, and insert blanks that indicate no activity!

You can write people's initials next to particular subtasks. Then you can easily see whose cooperation is needed or to whom you will delegate the entire subtask. For example, in writing an article, maybe you will charge one person with gathering all the research information before handing it off to you.

You can also use colors to help guide you along, whether the chart is on the wall, on a single piece of paper in a file folder, or on your hard drive. Green, for example, could be used to denote the start of tasks. Yellow could indicate some critical function. Blue could represent completion. Let your inner artist shine! Depending on the level of detail with which you are comfortable, you could devise separate milestone charts for each task.

If you're working with different people on each task, then a separate milestone chart might make it easier for them. Similarly, when you consider the broad range of priority areas in your life and the goals you've adopted in support of them, multiple milestone charts may seem preferable. Still, you want to keep things as simple as possible; otherwise, you'll need help organizing your organizing charts. And that's just another big mess to clean up.

	Item										
Task	1	2	3	4	5	6	7	8	9	10	11
Rewrite manual	»»»»	»»»»	»»»»								
Publish article		»»»»	»»»»	»»»»	»»»»	»»»»	»»»»	»»»»	»»»»	»»»»	»»»»
Interviews		»»									
Research		»»									
Organize			»								
Outline				»»							
1st draft						»»					
Peer Review						»»					
2nd draft								»»			
Submit								»			
Follow up											»
Online zine					»»»»	»»»»	»»»»	»»»»	»»»»		
DEF report						»»»»	»»»»				
Trade show							»»»				

29 **Flow by Using Charts** Most people have had experience with flow charts at one time or another, and for most it was not traumatic. No one I know spent thousands of dollars on therapy to work out their flow-chart-related angst. (If you have, please contact me.) Perhaps you remember an instance when one of your teachers in grade school drew a square, then drew a line to another square or circle, then down to yet another object. It could have been your math teacher depicting the relationship between numbers, your history teacher explaining the convoluted migration of nomadic peoples, your science teacher illuminating the interaction of chemical compounds, or your physical education teacher trying desperately to explain the oh-so-complicated game of kickball.

While flow charts are widely used to convey a process (how something happens), they are also quite convenient for helping you to:

- Track project progress
- Stay on target
- Accomplish your goals and stay organized

Flow charts can extend downward or to the right. In business, they usually extend to the right so that a timeline can be added to the top or bottom of the chart.

Flow charts are particularly useful in plotting activities related to a task or project area where many different people or resources may be required and where contingencies come into play. You can look at several possible outcomes with such a chart. If the answer to a question is yes, the flow chart proceeds along one path, and if the answer is no, it proceeds along another. Flow charts also allow for feedback loops. If an article is submitted to a publication and the editor wants specific changes, the feedback loop could

encompass where you go next. You can also buy erasable charts—
a valuable feature for making course corrections.

As with milestone charts, you can use colors, different shapes,
and symbols to convey different types of information at a glance.
If you add a key at the bottom of the chart that shows exactly
what each symbol and color represents, then you can't go wrong.
And your charts will look oh so pretty.

30 **Stay on Track** Using a calendar to ensure progress toward
chosen goals is a time-honored method of staying organized. If it was good enough for Julius Caesar, it's good enough
for you. Suppose one of your projects will be initiated and completed in the same calendar month. You are going to prepare a
completely new orientation manual for new hires. As the following
illustration indicates, the due date is March 30. So, on March 30
you write, "Complete manual."

To make this system work, use actual calendar pages from the
current year for however many months are relevant to the project
you are managing. If you haven't yet organized your desk, you may
want to post the calendar pages on the wall to avoid losing them.
Working from that end date back to the present, what needs to
take place right before you deliver the new orientation manual?

If eight working days prior to the deadline (March 22), you
need to meet with some department heads to offer your briefing
and obtain their input, then you schedule a conference on that day.

Likewise, you determine what needs to happen before the conference, as well as what comes directly after. In each case, plot the
dates on the calendar; then you could connect them with lines or
arrows that show the relationships of the dates. As in the case of
milestone charts and flow charts, you may use colors and symbols
to give you a quick visual review of your progress.

MARCH

Sunday	Monday	Tuesday	Wednesday	Thursday	Friday	Saturday
	1	2	3	4	5	6
7	8	9 *Initiate review*	10	11	12	13
14	15 *Proofread manual*	16	17	18	19 *Assemble copies*	20
21	22 *Schedule conference*	23	24	25	26	27
28	29	30 *Complete manual*	31			

With this calendar "Block-back" method, you can quickly see that if you miss any interim dates on the calendar in pursuit of successful completion of the project, then finishing subtasks at all other interim dates becomes jeopardized. Each interim date represents a mini-deadline. Hence, you have a built-in system for ensuring that your project will continue according to plan. Houston, we do *not* have a problem.

For goals that stretch on for years or decades, starting with the end in mind is the only practical way to proceed. Milestone charts, flow charts, and large wall calendars are available at office supply stores and their Web sites. So, go shopping!

31 **Clean Your Slate** When you have a place or space that you wish to organize, particularly if a little straightening up is long overdue, it often makes sense to clear the area completely before you proceed. If you're an outside sales representative, for example, in your car for much of the day, consider the case of your car's glove compartment! Your glove compartment might contain maps, an owner's manual, car registration materials, pens, pencils, paper, pennies, newspaper clippings, discount cards to restaurants, supermarket coupons and who knows what else.

How are you going to deal with such a mess? Empty the whole compartment, and put everything on the seat next to you. As you wade through the accumulation, toss the gum wrappers and other debris. Check the expiration dates on coupons, and chuck any that have expired. Keep the rest bound by a rubber band or paper clip.

Take the maps, car registration materials, and any other important documents, and lay them flat on the bottom of the glove compartment where they occupy the least space. Put back any items you deem essential such as tissues, pens and pencils, and other items that can lie reasonably flat. Put the discount coupons in last since those are items you'll want to review periodically.

Larger items that you want to keep in the glove compartment, such as a camera, medication, or gloves (hey, some people keep gloves in the glove compartment) go in last because they can rest comfortably on top of the aforementioned items.

Clearing out the glove compartment is easier than trying to organize it by sticking a hand or two deep into the mess and attempting to jostle things around. When everything is temporarily extracted, it becomes evident which items need not be replaced— plastic forks, for example. You also have a better opportunity to re-evaluate the need for long-standing items contained in your glove compartment. If you have four maps, but you've never used two of them, maybe those two can go in a folder in the trunk. Upon review, you could decide that the car is not the best place to store other items as well.

You might conclude that other items not previously kept in the glove compartment ought to be. In the storage space's newly organized state, there will be room for such items—until you let the glove compartment become totally disorganized again. (Just kidding; I know you're not going to let that happen any more.)

Use a "pay as you go" system—no ad hoc outposts, no accumulations, and no piles. Once you develop the habit of clearing space in all the compartments of your work and your life—your desk, your shelves, your car, closets, medicine cabinets, etc.—you accomplish many things. You demonstrate to yourself that you actually have the ability to stay organized, manage your affairs, and conduct your life; you remain in a ready state to handle what comes next rather than trying to merely squeak by!

Pretend It's Day One

When your places and spaces become too disorganized, pretend that it is "day one" and rearrange the area from scratch. This highly viable strategy works particularly well with the surface of your desk. Think back, for example, to when you assumed your current position at work. On day one, when you approached your office, cubicle, or other workspace, in what condition was the room, your desk, any nearby file cabinets, closets, and other spaces? Hopefully, empty. Imagine you're sitting down at your desk for the first time. Would you continue to include the items currently on it and would you place them in their current locations? If so, feel free to leave them where they are.

Reconsider the particulars of how you work with the materials in your office. Should some items be moved to the right or left?

Should anything be removed from the desktop? Does something need to be added? Consider every instance when you reach across the desk unnecessarily. If you're right-handed, consider the times you reach across to the left side for something. Can you rearrange all of your tools for economy of motion so that you do less maneuvering? Alternatively, are there items you prefer to have more than an arm's length away so that you will stretch throughout the course of a day?

Whatever you decide, the configuration of your desktop should suit the way you work and operate. Never mind what somebody else down the hall is doing! Adopt the "day one" mindset, and you may discover a desk and workspace arrangement that is novel for you, representing a boost in productivity and enjoyment.

32 **Defeat Desk Clutter** For the purpose of staying organized, as well as managing your time and feeling energized, clear your desk and surrounding area each evening as you end work for the day. Yes, you read it correctly—every evening before you depart. This will also help you start out at your best the next day.

I've discussed the issue of getting organized with top achievers in many different professions, including corporate executives, airline pilots, plant managers, and even fellow authors and speakers! Every person I questioned agrees that when his or her desk or office and personal surroundings are in order, he or she feels far more energized at the start of the day. Conversely, when these top achievers come into their offices at the start of the day and see a huge mess, they feel defeated.

Clearing your desk and surroundings each evening requires discipline. Most people don't want to clear their desks. It's a lot easier to simply depart for the day. You're tired, you're hungry, you miss your mom, I know. However, when you arrange your materials in the evening for higher productivity the next morning, a host of benefits come into play. When you leave with a clear desk, you give yourself a sense of closure or completion to your day.

When you arrive in the morning and find yourself greeted by neat, clean surroundings, you gain a psychological boost. What's more, you're either automatically drawn to the most important leftover issue, or you get to make a fresh decision about what materials to extract from your desk, file cabinet, or shelves based on what you want to accomplish that morning. This is often more productive than merely dealing with what you left on the desk the night before.

Some projects span several days, and for that reason it can be prudent on occasion to leave one (and only one!) file folder open on your desk so that it will catch your attention first thing the next morning. However, you don't want to fall into the habit of leaving unfinished piles on your desk each night. If you have one project, one file folder, or one of whatever you're working on in front of you, and the rest of your desk is clutter free, you are going to have:

- More energy
- More focus
- More direction
- More motivation

Consider the top of your desk, even if you can no longer see it through all the unkempt piles. (Quick, what color is your desktop?) What, precisely, do you need to have on it? A practical answer is: anything you use on a recurring and daily basis. This could include a pen, a roll of tape, a stapler, a staple remover, Post-it pads, a ruler, paper clips, and so on. Anything that you can't use on a daily or recurring basis does not belong on your desktop. Such items are best stored in a drawer within your desk, or possibly on a table or credenza behind you.

Why bother to make the distinction between what you use on a daily or recurring basis and what you don't? Because your goal at all times is to have as much open space as possible to support the way you work. You want clear, clean, flat surfaces. You literally need a disembarking area—a place where you can open packages and break down the mail, thereby diminishing piles and accumulations.

Examples of Useful Items for Your Desk

- Paper
- Letterhead
- Business envelopes
- Letter opener
- Stamps
- Ruler
- Stapler and staple remover
- Scissors
- Business cards
- Drawer dividers
- Tissues
- Pens, pencils, highlighters, and felt-tip pens
- Markers
- Note cards and greeting notes
- Scratch paper and Post-it pads
- Paper clips

Place supporting and familiar items near your desk, but not on it. This includes personal objects, such as pictures, plants, and personal motivators. Also, if an item enhances your productivity, efficiency, and creativity, place it near, but not on, your desk. Okay, maybe you can keep a few small, personal items on your desk, such as pictures or toys.

Useful Tools for Surrounding Areas
- File folders
- Large wastebasket
- Bulletin board

These are tools that you will need on hand when you are mailing, filing, and engaging in other routine office chores. Long-life stampers, which can be printed with "Draft" or "Review and Return," help reduce the time you spend writing by hand when organizing and sending out materials.

Hereafter, manage your desk surface as if it's one of the most important elements to staying organized, because it is. Recognize that when you begin each morning with a clear, organized desk and a clean, organized office, you work with more energy, focus, direction, and motivation. It becomes easier to concentrate on the tasks that you deem most important and urgent.

What's Inside Counts
Inside your desk retain items that you use on a weekly basis, although items used daily can be stored there, too. Recognize, however, that your desk drawers are not for storing supplies. You may retain a pad of paper, but not pads of paper. You only need one pad at a time; you're not opening your own office supply store . . . are you?

The guiding principle is to have an item inside your desk if and when you periodically need it. Keep pads of paper and other extra supplies in a file folder, a storage locker, or in some other space away from the epicenter of your creative and productive post.

If you choose to use one of your desk drawers to contain file folders, then ensure that the file folders all represent current projects. Place the important and urgent materials at the front and the least important and least urgent materials at the back.

Routinely discard extraneous information, and be on the lookout for opportunities to reduce, shrink, and pare down the piles. Files are most useful when there are only important documents inside, so retain only the materials that are essential. Carefully assess whether or not your multiyear collection of Chinese restaurant takeout menus should make the cut.

Once you have only those things on your desktop that ought to be on your desktop, and only those items in your desk that ought to be in your desk, proceed to the other storage compartments around your office. You can do it!

33 **Show Your Shelves Who's Boss** You probably have some type of shelving in your office, cubicle, or work station. The issue of what to house on your shelves versus what is best contained in a file cabinet is relatively easy to address. Essentially, shelves are best used to do the following:

- Temporarily store items you are bound to use within ten to fifteen days
- Store items that are too large to fit in a file cabinet
- Present a collection of like items, such as twelve issues of the same magazine, in an upright magazine storage box
- House projects in progress
- Store books, directories, supply catalogs, and other items with spine labels

Items you are temporarily storing on shelves are ideally used in ten to fifteen days; they don't hang around for forty to sixty or more days. It's exceedingly easy to lose track of this. Once a temporary pile becomes a semi-permanent file, you begin to lose control of what you're retaining. Clutter in your office starts to mount, and you wonder again why you feel so disorganized!

Be careful as well when storing elements of a project-in-progress on your shelves. It's fine to temporarily park the brunt of materials you are working with so that you only have a few materials before you on your desk at any given time. However, if you're maintaining an orderly desk, then the project materials at hand should rotate from your desk to the shelf and back to your desk. The mass of materials needs to get thinner in the process and eventually not appear on your shelves at all.

The Lighter the Load, the Better

As more and more stuff floods into your office, you'll find it's no feat to fill up your shelves in record time. All the office supply catalogs, annual directories, software instruction guides, and company policy and procedure manuals contribute to quickly turn an open space into a "no vacancy" situation. This is why it is crucial to keep supplies in an actual supply cabinet. Imagine that.

Supply cabinets are designed to house items in bulk. These items might be stacked on top of one another, placed horizontally, or end to end. Ideally, your supply cabinet is farther away from your desk than your shelves. While you want to strive to arrange items on your shelves with precision, supply cabinets allow for more leeway.

The primary benefit of using supply cabinets is that you are able to open them and readily find what you need. It helps if you keep like items together. However, extreme neatness is only marginally important here. If you're in a small office, as long as all employees can find what they need within the supply cabinet, it is probably okay.

The bigger the office staff sharing the same supply cabinet, the more important neatness becomes. So, once again, neatness counts, as your third-grade teacher used to say.

Interconnectedness

Organized individuals eventually grasp that the relationship between one's desk, shelves, and supply cabinet is not static. What is housed in one location ultimately may be housed somewhere else, depending on the following:

- The tasks at hand
- The available resources to meet those tasks
- The time frame

Like a cat hot on the trail of a rodent, always be on the prowl for what can be tossed or recycled. If you don't need some item or haven't looked at it since the day you acquired it, the item is probably not worth filing or storing. Too many people feel fearful about tossing items, however, because they know they will "need it the next day." "I know the moment I toss something . . ." This is not nearly as great a problem as one might imagine in the digital age.

Nearly any list, report, or document that you can name can be replaced. Somebody else has a copy; it's on the Internet; or it's on somebody's hard drive. If you can't think of a good reason to hang on to something, that is an excellent reason to toss it. Don't become a pack rat; the world is already full of them.

Many executives retain information at work only to tuck it away, never to be used again. Organizing pundits proclaim that 80 percent of what you file is never used again. Even if the pundits are off by 25 to 50 percent in their estimates, it still means that much of what you are hanging on to could be deadwood. The more you clear out your office, the easier it is to find the important things that you've actively chosen to retain.

34 **Gain Power over Paper** Milt knew that he needed to get organized, but he let years pass without addressing the issue. He would do anything but straighten his files. Then, when he needed to find something, he spent untold hours rummaging around and was never in control. Milt could not be trusted to return anything. This reputation hampered his career and working relationships. It probably restricted his earnings. . . . Need I say more?

If you analyzed your most repetitive task, chances are that handling paper would top the list on most days. In many respects, getting organized is synonymous with paper handling!

Knowing where to find things, such as necessary papers, files, and other documents, is a sign of competence and provides a measure of freedom to concentrate on creative, fulfilling work rather than on the clutter that surrounds you. Unfortunately, career professionals today, like poor Milty, are plagued by more paper than their predecessors of a generation ago, despite the long-standing promise that we'd all be working in "paperless offices."

There's little wonder that it's so easy to become disorganized, in record time, considering the volume of paper everyone handles daily. A Pitney Bowes study indicated that from 2000 to 2004, annual catalog sales grew at 6.7 percent compared with 4.5 percent for total retail sales. Figures from the U.S. Postal Service reveal that last year more than 19.5 billion catalogs were mailed in the United States—that's the equivalent of sixty-four catalogs for every man, woman, and child, including newborns, in America. If you retain all of those catalogs, no wonder you're buried in paper!

Despite the popularity of e-mail, the Direct Marketing Association reports that the growth rate in the total volume of regular, third-class, bulk mail (fondly known as junk mail) continues to increase at a pace faster than growth rate in the population. The typical executive receives at least 175 pieces of unsolicited mail each month. I've calculated that the average person spends a total of eight solid months of his or her life reading junk mail.

Greenpeace, an organization dedicated to protecting the environment, at one point was annually sending out 25 million pieces of direct mail to its huge database of members, supporters, and prospects. So much for being green. Today, they're presumably sending less mail and relying more on door-to-door, grassroots efforts.

Your mission is to whittle down all those pages of catalogs, magazines, and other voluminous materials that come your way so that you deal with only what you need. You can avoid being besieged with paper by reducing the potential for disorganization from the start, such as the moment when:

- You receive the daily mail
- Somebody hands you something
- Something is placed in your inbox

Use your copier as often as possible to retain the few pages you need from a book or other item. Scan key paragraphs and pages directly onto your hard drive, where it will be easily searchable and retrievable via your various word-processing functions. This is superior to filing something, then seeking to find it on your own. A word of caution: Don't make the mistake of overscanning, or you'll fill up your hard drive as haphazardly as you filled up your file cabinets. Your computer will not be happy with you and will fight back by hiding files, which will stress you even more and perpetuate the vicious cycle. Disorganization, either electronic or manual, is equally anxiety provoking.

Use a junk drawer as a holding bin when stuff comes to you too quickly, such as when you're in the middle of an important project, or when you simply "can't deal with that right now." Later, when you have an opportunity, go to your junk drawer, and plow through it as much as you can. Then, use this four-step process for assessing where the items will go:

1. Act on it
2. Delegate it
3. File it
4. Recycle or toss it

That's it!

Rank the items in your thin "act on it" file according to what is important and urgent, moving down to what is unimportant and not urgent. Understandably, this category ought to always be the smallest.

Questions That Count

If it helps, ask yourself a series of questions that can help you quickly determine what to do with the next item that crosses your desk. These include questions such as:

- What does this document represent?
- Is there any reason to retain this?
- Who else needs to know about this?

If an item you receive merits your attention and actually requires you to get back in touch with someone, use the path of least resistance to resolve the issue. In other words, try to:

- Fax instead of mail
- E-mail instead of fax
- Pay by credit card or debit card instead of by check
- Pay online
- Call instead of visit

Continually Be on the Lookout

Throughout the day, when the spirit moves you, examine your desktop, desk drawers, shelves, file cabinet, and storage cabinet to determine what, if anything, no longer needs to be retained. This includes outdated directories or instruction manuals you know you're not going to use again. Also identify any outdated fly-ers, annual reports, PR materials, announcements, catalogs, and invitations. Gentle hint: If you don't find anything, go back and search for real!

Feel free to chuck old editions of books that you'll never open again. You can also throw away back issues of magazines that you haven't touched for more than a year or two. Better yet, recycle them. Organizing your desk and helping the environment—look at you go!

Get rid of scraps, rough drafts, memos, correspondence, reports, and any documents that do not have to be retained. Chuck the excess vendor supply catalogs that you may have on hand, as well as duplicate items, annual reports that you don't look at, soft-ware you received in the mail that you are never going to explore, and take-out restaurant menus for places you haven't ordered from this decade.

35 **Smile While You File** Filing is the ultimate organizational technique, which is unwelcome news to some. When you file items intelligently, you enable yourself to efficiently withdraw what you need when you need it. As Jim Cathcart, author of *The Acorn Principle*, says, "Filing is not about storing, it is about retrieval." You file things because either they will help you to be prosperous in the future (the information you retain has power), or because there are penalties for not filing (you won't be able to complete your taxes). Thus all items that you file should have some potential future value. When it comes to organizing files, the popular choice is to park them in a file cabinet—preferably one with doors that open and close easily.

Start with a two-drawer file cabinet that is about 18 to 24 inches in length. You probably won't need anything larger, especially now that you understand the beauty of keeping only what is necessary. Use colored file folders to separate items in order to give you visual control of your drawer.

Think of the last time you were in your doctor's office. If the doctor's patient files were exposed, chances are you saw some kind of color-coded filing system. This kind of system enables the office staff to go right to the appropriate area, which cuts down on the time spent searching for any particular file. Color-coded files help you find things more quickly and easily. You could assign green file folders for anything that has to do with, say, money, blue for anything that has to do with your career progression, yellow for anything related to taxes, and so on.

Desk drawers can also serve as file cabinets, although the space is limited. Unless the desk is well designed, it is often difficult to easily open and close the drawer. Storing the information that you file and extract on a regular basis nearby is convenient, and I recommend it.

If you find that the files are becoming voluminous, with little slack in the drawers, first prune what you can. Chuck old and obsolete papers, duplicates, and anything else you feel that you don't need to retain. The moment you have to stuff files to force them into the drawer, and pull with considerable tug to extract them, it's a reasonable bet that there is a file cabinet in your future. As long as you have about 20 percent of your desk drawer vacant, you're in decent shape.

If it's been about a half millennium since you organized your file cabinet, rather than attempt to redo the whole thing, tackle only half a drawer every week. This will keep you at a safe and sane pace. Assemble the tools you'll need to be effective, such as several blank file folders, file folder labels, markers, and anything else that supports your efforts. You may also need to use color-coded dots, a stapler, paper clips, fasteners, sticky pads, and other organizing tools. Rather than using two or three manila folders, feel free to splurge—employ black, green, pink, orange, or blue folders.

Grab the first file in the drawer you have chosen to tackle. Examine its contents.

- What can be combined?
- What needs to be reallocated?
- What color folder or what color label will you use to house the remaining materials?

Everything in the file is subject to being combined, deleted, or moved around. Your goal at all times is to ensure that the things you have chosen to file are housed in their best possible location.

Go into the second file in the drawer, whip through it the same way, and allocate its contents. If you're not sure that something is worth retaining, chances are it's not worth retaining, since most of us have a tendency to over-retain and over-file. Chances are astronomically high that you can safely pare down a good chunk of your files and suffer no consequences. As always, the less you have, the easier it is to find that which you chose to retain. Less is more!

When you have gone through your half drawer, relax, give yourself a break, and go do something else. You don't have to tackle the second half of the drawer until a week or so from now. You're relieved, I know.

Fewer Files, More in Them

Always seek to have fewer large files of like items as opposed to a larger number of smaller files. Why? You'll find it easier to extract what you are seeking if you only have to deal with a few large files to begin with. You will find the right file with ease, since there are only a few choices. It will then take you time to go through that file to find the particular document, but your odds of success will be high because you have already confined your search to a specific area.

Conversely, if you have dozens and dozens of small files, you might not extract the correct file even after three or four tries. Guessing games are no fun when it to comes to extracting what you need. If you are lucky, and you do locate the correct file, the time required to find the desired page within the file won't be that much less than if you had pulled the desired page from a larger file.

Many people have been able to reduce paper handling by employing a program like Barbara Hemphill's Paper Tiger software, available at *www.thepapertiger.com*. It enables users to readily access files and eliminate duplications without having to scan hundreds (ugh) of documents.

Some people swear by date stamping. Every time something goes into your file, you stamp the corner of it indicating on what day it was placed in the file. If you're comfortable with doing this, go ahead. However, it's okay if you don't. Usually, an item's importance is not related to the date on which you filed it, although the longer an item has lingered in your files without ever being used, the higher the probability that you can safely chuck it.

What you file and how you file is largely governed by the file headings—the labels you place on the tab section of each file folder. It is easy enough to label one file folder "Office Supplies," and another "Personal Documents," but you want to be creative in your labeling to accommodate the gaggle of stuff that comes your way. You'll probably find that some of the influx doesn't seem to have a proper home. Who is to say that you cannot label your file folders with the following?

- Review this after the first of the year
- Hold until after the merger
- Check in one month
- Review next spring
- Don't know where to file

By having a file labeled "Don't Know Where to File," you automatically create a home for the handful of things that your instincts tell you to retain or that you just can't bear to part with, but which don't fit anything else that you're doing. Now, at least you have a fair chance of getting your hands back on such items when, lo and behold, the time might be right to reread them closely.

Don't worry that a file labeled "Don't Know Where to File" may grow too large too quickly. You always have the opportunity to open that file quickly, review its contents, and make decisions regarding what you see—acting, delegating, refiling, or tossing it. When you review a refiled item a second or third time, you can almost automatically toss it. So, get your wastebasket ready.

36 **Tickle Your Fancy with Tickler Files** There are extreme benefits to setting up a daily and monthly "rotating tickler file." Suppose something crosses your desk in March—it looks interesting, but you don't have to act on it until April 25. If you have one file folder for each month of the year, January to December, you can park the item in the April folder.

Going further, you could set up an additional thirty-one file folders marked #1 through #31. (Or thirty or twenty-eight, and don't forget about twenty-nine on leap years!) Now, when April comes around, you open up the April file folder, take out all the contents, and allocate the items to file folders #1 through #31 as appropriate. You stick the April file folder at the end of the pack, so that the month of May is now in front, preceded by the file folders for the individual days of the current month.

These forty-three file folders, #1 through #31 and January through December, allow you to park anything in the appropriate place when the item doesn't have to be dealt with too soon. If you receive something on the third day of the month, but you don't have to deal with it until the eighteenth of the month, put it in the folder marked the eighteenth, or better yet, to give yourself some slack, put it in a folder labeled two or three days before the due date.

When you institute tickler files, much of the clutter and stuff on your desk and around your office will immediately gain a home, because you've set a date when you're going to review the materials. They are off your desk, off your counters, and off your mind.

Yet, you haven't lost them. You have simply placed them in a location where you'll be able to retrieve them at a time when it makes the most sense to deal with them.

You can use a tickler file to write your checks and pay your bills, and then store the envelopes in the appropriate folder prior to sending. Many people who use tickler files find it convenient to review them at the start of each week, and perhaps one or two more times during that week. One of the benefits of this system is that when you review an item days, weeks, or months after first putting it in the tickler file, you often have a greater sense of objectivity. Choosing to act on it, delegate it, refile it, or toss it becomes easier. Happily, much of what you review gets tossed. Thus, you'll find less clutter, greater organization, and greater focus and direction in terms of the pressing tasks that you face. Isn't that why you're here?

You can also set up electronic "tickler" reminders by employing the calendar function in computer programs. That way you can stay on top of important projects, deadlines, and not mess up on birthdays, gift giving, and other personal touches.

Creating Files in Advance of the Need
A variation on the theme of employing both file labels and tickler files is creating files in advance of the actual need to store anything in them. Suppose you've decided that you absolutely want to work in the London office of your company by the end of next year. Perhaps you haven't even announced your intentions to anyone. Nevertheless, place a file in your file cabinet labeled "London," or set up a file folder on your hard disk similarly labeled.

Every time you see something about London, hereafter, instead of placing it in a random folder, you now have an easily accessible location. Maybe you have documents from the London office that you want to file, or there is something you want to hold on to related to travel planning. Later, perhaps you come across something related to housing that you'll want to keep as a reference.

You can create several hardcopy or computer file folders in advance based on the priorities you have identified and the goals you have established in support of those priorities. Here are some ideas for file folders of this kind:

- Insurance plans
- Equipment acquisition
- Benefits packages
- Vacation to Bali
- Digital cameras
- Grants and awards

Creating a file folder in advance of having anything to put into the folder affirms the goals you have chosen. At the least, it helps keep you organized. If you don't have such a folder, where are you going to put all of your papers? On top of a pile where it will be buried by whatever is placed on top? That's not a good idea.

The value of preemptive file folders obviously is no less valid when it comes to organizing your hard drive. There may be a half dozen or so file folders that would be most appropriate for you to create based on where you are heading in your career and your life. When you create an empty file folder on your hard drive, especially when it's accessible off of another folder that you visit often, you automatically gain a convenient reminder that you do indeed have a home for files as they emerge for this new topic area.

The tickler system works particularly well if you supervise a small staff of employees. Create a file folder for each person and name it for him or her. You can even create a file for yourself on your hard drive called "In Progress" that you open at the start of each day. The possibilities are endless! The point is for you to create space to house files so that you can quickly and easily retrieve what you need when you choose to. Everything needs a home, even your files!

Look upon establishing tickler files and files in advance of need as easy ways to become efficient in handling paper. Remain a lean and mean organizing machine. Keep your files thin but potent. Rather than seeing filing as drudgery, consider it a vital key to an organized career and life.

37 **Pick Apart Your Piles** Despite all of your sterling efforts, you may be among those who find themselves continually confronted with visible signs of disorganization, such as piles and clutter. Take heart. The situation is not hopeless. Piles and clutter didn't magically accumulate (or did they?) and they don't magically go away. First, gather all the tools you may need to enable you to break down those piles or disband that clutter. Such tools could include file folders, rubber bands, paper clips, staplers, boxes, and so on.

Allow yourself thirty minutes, or if that's too much, fifteen minutes, to go through each item in the pile and assess what might best be done with it.

Recall the simple system for organizing things in tip #34. You have four options when confronting what to do with all of your stuff. You can:

- Act on it
- Delegate it
- File it
- Recycle or toss it

Do you remember it? Good.

If you look through any given pile of stuff on your desk, chances are that most of it can be recycled. You don't need to hang on to much of the contents. A lesser portion can probably be filed, and a slightly lesser portion of that can probably be delegated. That leaves you, hopefully, with a thin stack of items to act upon. With such organizing activity, when you stop and critically examine a pile or accumulation, you stand a better chance of whittling out the unnecessary and dealing with the rest (which usually represents a manageable amount).

For files on your hard drive, a variety of software programs are available, such as Time Saver Wolf at *www.lonewolf-software.com,* which allow users to prioritize information. This software offers a "category tree" system that allows you to create, edit, rename, and move categories as your little heart desires.

As you break down accumulated piles, don't spend too much time deciding where to place each item: either in your new "act on it" pile, "delegate it" pile, "file it" pile, or "recycle or toss it" pile. Make a quick assessment and go to the next item.

Once your four new piles are complete, undoubtedly . . . hopefully . . . you will notice that the "recycle or toss it" pile is the largest. The "file it" pile, we can only pray, will be much smaller. The pile of stuff to delegate to other people is smaller still, and the file of things you need to act on is characteristically the smallest of all—lucky you!

Of those items that you need to act on, if you have six items competing for your time and attention, the most effective and efficient approach is to mercilessly mow them down one by one. They won't get jealous. After all, you can't be in six places at once, and neither can your brain! Rank the items according to their importance, and work on number one to completion, or as far as you can take it, then proceed to number two, and so on. No other approach to handling six important and urgent items competing for your attention works as well as the method described here.

Proceed, then, through the items that you need to act on, and rank them according to what is most important. If an item is both important and urgent, put it at the top of the pile. If it is important but not urgent, place it next. If it is simply urgent, place it after that. Finally, if it is neither urgent nor important, recycle, file, or delegate it. You'd be amazed at how many items belong in this category, such as specialized course offerings, new product announcements, or an article on management theory that goes on and on.

To launch into high gear, start tackling the items on the top of the pile that has the items you have decided are important and urgent. If you put the single most important and urgent item on top, the second in second place, the third in third place, and so forth, you are ready for high productivity.

Tackling the Important Pile

Once you're ready to begin working on the items in your important pile, list them all along with an estimate of how long it will take to complete each item. Then, add all the estimates together and multiply that number by 1.5. This compensates for your underestimation. Let's face it, things often take longer than we originally conceive. I mean, is this news? We don't know how long a project will take until we actually engage in it.

If the number of task hours you face to complete the important pile grows to an astronomical figure, don't blow a mental fuse. It's not that the challenge has necessarily changed; you simply have better information regarding it. Marshal your resources accordingly. Contemplate what it will take to accomplish all that you have laid out before you as important and urgent, important, and so on. You may need additional staff help, or a bigger budget. In the short run, you may need to work longer hours. (Sorry, but it's true. On the bright side, it might save you time or stress in the future.)

Sometimes you can't take a task all the way to completion. Maybe it requires help from others. Perhaps you need someone else to approve certain steps. Progress as far as you can go, then consult with others. During the interim, however, start on the next project. Similarly, proceed with it as far as you can go—to completion if you can.

Now and then, no matter how methodical your approach or well organized your desk or office, newly introduced items will compete for your time and attention and conspire to upset your perfectly arranged kingdom. Such occurrences are expected—on a daily, if not hourly, basis. Will it ever stop?

As time passes, you'll find that you need a break from working on the important tasks that you have so carefully arranged. Again, this happens to everyone. You can only give your rapt attention and earnest efforts to the primo projects for so long, and then your mind starts to wander. You need a mental break. At this point, turn to items of lesser significance that don't require as much mental effort. When you feel ready, return to the most important items, which are still situated conveniently on the top of the pile.

Continually strive to keep your piles as slim and trim as possible. Put those fatties on a diet! You want to reduce the weight and volume of each pile by retaining only the highly relevant information and nothing more. For example, rather than keeping a ten-page report, hang on to only the single page that you actually need.

Taking this practice further, if you only need one paragraph, phone number, address, or Web site, clip that specific portion and recycle the rest of the page. Attach the small clipping that you have retained to a sheet that contains other small relevant tidbits. Then, lay the assemblage down on the copier machine. You now have a dossier page that fully supports what you are working on but doesn't take up much physical or psychological space.

Sometimes it does pay to let piles or accumulations mount up, *temporarily*. When you receive a plethora of similar items, it's okay to let the pile grow for a while. Perhaps a stack of everything related to the competitor's product is accumulating on the corner table in your office. The pile is temporary, and you intend to handle it completely, soon.

When that sacred time arrives, delve into the pile like a buzz saw through balsa wood. Discard duplicate information immediately. Combine like items, and consider which can be recycled, as well. Pare down so that you have the slimmest, most potent file possible. When the pile is reasonably thin, peruse it again. Is there anything else that can be thrown out? I thought so!

38 **Pare Down and Persevere** You can plan your day with the skill and precision of a surgeon, without even going to medical school. Despite all the techniques discussed so far, at some point in the day, mail, e-mail, Web sites, or phone calls will intrude. You will be accosted by material to be read, learned, or otherwise acted upon, thus throwing you off schedule. Each new intrusion can consume a few minutes or several hours. Added to everything else you're balancing, even small amounts of additional information can bring on feelings of frustration and anxiety.

How can you pare down a little at a time without breaking your stride? When you've finished a big project at work and you're not in the mindset to tackle some other major, intellectual challenge at the moment, pare down your holdings as a form of transition.

For example, if you recently finished a big report:

- Can you update any logs and reporting forms?
- Are there any memos or documents to send as a result of the finished report?
- Can you get rid of rough drafts and notes that are no longer applicable (notes you'll never use again)?

Be on the lookout for ways to continually pare down your accumulations. *Kaizen,* meaning continuous improvement, is an essential part of a Japanese philosophy about how to approach work. The seasoned kaizen practitioner seeks ways to make improvements that offer the most immediate and dramatic paybacks. Veterans know that such results prompt one to look for even more ways to improve. The art of seeking continuous improvement is challenging, and in many cases, fun. If your plans turn awry because it's pouring and the bridge is out, or the plane has been delayed for an hour and ten minutes, in what tiny ways can you engage in continual improvement? You can always pare down!

Despite the availability of all manner of electronic gadgetry, I know high-powered executives who will have none of it. "None of it, I tell you!" Their airplane seat, they say, is among the few sanctuaries they have. It's where they get to open their briefcases and plow through them from A to Z, merging and purging, updating lists, chucking what is no longer necessary, and whipping that little "office in the air" back into shape.

The same holds true if you commute by rail or bus. Use the brief moments of the day to pare down. Instead of lugging around heavy issues of *Forbes, BusinessWeek*, or the *Wall Street Journal*, for example, extract only the articles that appear relevant to you. Merely reducing the volume of paper confronting you invariably is not the end-all to your organizational challenge. However, having addressed this issue as an author, professional speaker, and certified management consultant (CMC) for twenty-three years, I'm convinced that reducing paper volume is a tremendous boon to any quest to becoming organized. A slimmer file is easier to handle. Fewer notes in front of you mean fewer notes to contemplate. Fewer, but highly relevant, research materials means less time reading, digesting, and applying what you have assembled. Any way you cut it, when you pare down, you increase the probability of succeeding in your organization quest.

Continue to Prune Your Files

The time and effort that you spend whittling what you no longer need pays off in many ways. For one, you physically have the space both within your desk and file cabinets and on your hard drive to accommodate new information, which, as we know, is well on its way. Chucking what you don't need gives you the opportunity to review that which you have filed and choose to retain:

- Contacts logged into your database may have left the area, perhaps passed away, or are no longer relevant based on your priorities and goals. Delete them without remorse from your database.
- Likewise, you can toss every slip of paper in your files relating to issues that aren't important, urgent, or interesting. Keep the others in the aforementioned holding bin, or place them where you park stuff that doesn't need to be seen or dealt with for now.
- On your hard drive, eliminate items that formerly captured your attention, but now, after months or perhaps years, have overstayed their welcome.

- Examine your office. Are there gifts and mementos you have received that hold little meaning for you or take up more space than they are worth? Are there books, reports, documents, and other items for which you still do not know the value? The following chart offers a quick look at what to retain versus what to toss:

Item	Feel Free to Toss or Recycle if . . .	Feel Free to Retain if . . .
Business cards, notes	You have many cards and never call anyone, or you can't recall the person, or the goods or services provided.	You already have a cardholder, can scan it, know you'll use it, or feel you will.
Papers, files, and documents	It's old, outdated, or uninformative; it's been transferred to disk.	It's your duty to retain it, you refer to it often, it has future value, or it comforts you.
Reports, magazines	It's old, outdated, stacking up, you think you need it to keep up, or you fear a quiz on it.	It's vital to your career or well-being, you choose to retain it, or there will be a quiz on it.
Books, guides, directories	You've copied, scanned, or made notes on the key pages, it's obsolete, or has an updated version.	It's a part of a life collection, you refer to it monthly, it has sentimental value, or you want it.
CDs, DVDs, videos, cassettes	You never play it, or if you do, it doesn't evoke any feelings or memories. It plays poorly.	You play it, you like it, you couldn't bear to part with it. It's a keepsake.
Mementos, memorabilia	It no longer holds meaning, you have many similar items, you do not have room, and you've changed.	It still evokes strong memories, you will hand it down someday, or it looks good on display.
Gifts, cards, presents	It's never in use, not wanted, and the bestowed won't know or be concerned that you tossed it.	You use it often, are glad you have it, or are saving it for some special reason.

39 **Can Your Spam, Junk Your Junk Mail** E-mail is a growing problem for practically everyone. My guru on managing e-mail and controlling spam is Wayne McKinnon, author of *The Complete Guide to E-mail*.

Wayne contends that if you have to sort through hundreds of messages each time you seek information, your search will be inefficient. What's more, many of your stored messages become redundant the moment you receive a current message.

It's easier to stay organized, as you proceed in a pay-as-you-go fashion, than to face a daunting number of unsorted messages. If you choose to store your messages locally rather than on your organization's e-mail server, then you and you alone are responsible to back up those files.

If you start each day by reading new mail, delegate what you can before you respond. You may often find that others can tend to the tasks better or provide you with useful information to help you respond. Most people, most of the time, just want an answer, and they don't care where the heck it comes from!

Not all messages are equal, so mark your messages with the proper priority. Messages from customers and your boss generally are important and may be urgent. Read those messages before the rest of your inbox. Since many e-mail systems allow you to mark an urgency level on the messages you send, encourage your colleagues and any staff to use this feature appropriately.

Filter out the Crap

E-mail software offers sophisticated filtering systems. By establishing specific rules, you can automatically sort, respond to, and delete messages. If you constantly receive junk mail from a certain address, set up a filter that will file or delete any message they send to you. You already know this, but are you using your filter to best advantage? Use your filters to maintain a list of your top-priority contacts, direct everything else out of your inbox, and weed out unwelcome known addresses. Also use your filters to examine message text, look for common phrases, and discard the inane. Play around to find what works for you depending on the types of messages you receive.

Here's something worth heeding: Prevent your address from being picked up by trolling bots by making it invisible to them. Bots and worms can't gather what they can't see, so here's how to keep them in the dark. Change your format. For example, my e-mail address *Jeff@BreathingSpace.com* can alternatively be written as Jeff(at)BreathingSpace.com.

This format appears enough like a standard e-mail address for most people to understand, but the bots will pass right over it. The downside is that if people want to get in touch with you they cannot simply click on your e-mail address. Instead, they will have to compose a message manually and enter your proper address.

The Paper Chase

What about good old hard-copy paper? How often should you handle a piece of paper? I say that it always depends on what the paper says. When you make a purchase by mail, your name is sold and circulated to dozens of catalog houses. Some organizations repeatedly send huge amounts of junk mail, which wastes your time and clutters your life. Just ask anyone who recently turned eighteen and immediately was accosted by everyone from Avon, to Discover, to the U.S. Army. A gross offender is an organization that believes it has a God-given duty to continually inundate you with catalogs, brochures, and junk mail. Such parties merit special attention. If your name gets into the mailing list system, they're not likely to set you free. Don't be their prisoner! You need to apply strong medicine to those who would impede your desire to pare down, uncomplicate your life, and stay in control:

- When you're besieged by third-class mail from repeat or gross offenders, and such offenders have included a self-addressed bulk mail reply envelope, use the envelope to request that your name be removed from their lists. Also, review their literature or Web site to see if there is an 800 number you can use to make such a request at no cost.

- For those who don't heed your request, file a complaint with the Direct Marketing Association (DMA), the U.S. Postal Service, and the Office of the General Counsel of the offending group. After all, in an era when each piece of mail adds to environmental glut, it's your civic duty, as well as an effective technique for achieving breathing space, to reduce the amount of junk mail you receive. The DMA claims you can eliminate a sizable chunk of your junk mail with a Web site visit to *www.dmachoice.org/consumerassistance.php*. Follow the links and fill in the requested information accordingly.

To further aid you in seeking to stay off of mailing lists from a repeat or gross offender, here are more tips to beating junk mail. You'll thank me later.

- When making any mail order purchase, feel free to mention or include a preprinted label that reads, "I don't want my name placed on any mailing lists whatsoever, and forbid the use, sale, rental, or transfer of my name." Internet sites often include an option like this on their Web page, but it is often hard to find or in a small font size. They're tricky, aren't they?

- Sometimes the fastest way to deal with repeat offenders is to write the words "speed reply" right on the communication you've received. Underneath those two words write the message, "Please remove me from your mailing list now and forever." Sign your name, date it, and send back the same items or communication that you received. Be sure to address it to the mailing list manager of the offending organization.
- You can fight junk mail by saving all of it for weeks. Then hand it to an administrative aide at work and ask to have each group put on notice. Or, on your own, hire a high school student at minimum wage to send a form letter to every party who has sent you mail more than once. Explain carefully that you have no interest in their offer.
- Some vendors ask for your name and address even when you pay in cash. Feel free to respectfully decline.
- At all times and in all places, inform the parties with whom you do business that you do not appreciate having your name added to mailing lists, or being inundated by catalogs, announcements, brochures, and fliers. This is necessary if you place an order by fax, make a purchase by credit card, fill out a magazine subscription form, or procure any other type of good or service.

40 **Proceed to Read** Undoubtedly, reading has become a major issue for you. The amount of reading you fathom to stay informed, further your career, or amuse yourself can be staggering. When you add it up, the piles can be daunting. In the course of a week you may find yourself spending anywhere from ten to twenty hours simply on reading.

How can anyone today manage to stay organized in our overwhelming information society? Fortunately, there are several techniques you can employ to assist you in completing your reading more swiftly, to help you organize what you need to retain, and still feel as if you have a life.

If you have some familiarity with what you are reading, even a somewhat noisy place can be an adequate environment but, in general, the quieter the place you find, the faster and easier you will be able to read and reflect. Find a quiet sanctuary particularly whenever you are reading about highly technical issues, subjects unfamiliar to you, heavy philosophical pieces, or anything the prompts you to pause and reflect before proceeding. It's too difficult to do this kind of reading when you are surrounded by distractions.

You probably already know the value of reading early in the morning before others come into your office, or perhaps even earlier, before you leave your house. The same holds true for the evening, after everyone has left the office, or at home, after everyone else has retired. You can read faster and more thoroughly at these times.

Employ these techniques to improve your comprehension and speed:

- *Skimming.* Looking at the first couple of sentences of each paragraph within an article or chapter in a book is called skimming. By skimming you get to quickly find out whether you should read the article or chapter in greater depth. Simply skimming the first sentence or two is often all you need to gain the essence of the information being provided. Remind you of college at all?
- *Scanning.* If you encounter a large volume of reading, such as a sizable book or a large report, it's not often practical to attempt skimming. With scanning, you quickly learn enough about the document to determine if it merits

even greater attention. Scanning involves reviewing any list, chart, or exhibit in the book, the index, the table of contents, some of the chapter titles, the foreword, and summaries.

Often, you can identify the handful of relevant passages or pages that are worth photocopying through scanning, and then recycle the remainder of the book or report. By the way, copying for limited, personal use does not violate copyright law. If you're reading a PDF file or e-book, print only those pages most valuable to you. This prevents creating an even larger pile.

- *Evaluating the source.* The best sources routinely provide the best information. Rather than plow through dozens of industry journals, pick the best two or three, extracting articles of importance. You'll reduce the total volume of what you need to read, while ensuring that you're being exposed to the latest of what's occurring in your industry or profession. Online, this can be even easier. If you're reading an e-journal or online newspaper or e-zine, search for keywords that interest you, thereby conveniently finding those articles of most interest. Sometimes the computer really can save time!
- *Assemble your tools.* If you use sticky pads, paper clips, felt-tip pens, highlighters, scissors, and the like to assist you in your efforts when you read, then have them nearby. When you can deftly extract or highlight information you wish to retain, the overall reading burden is greatly reduced. Then you can maintain a lean, mean, potent file consisting of information and items that you will actually act upon or maybe retain.

- *Cut books down to size.* Do you lament your lack of opportunity to tackle some of the current full-length books available? Unquestionably, there will be more full-length books than you have the time or inclination to read. Here is an organized method for approaching them in a highly productive manner:
  - Read the back jacket in detail first. In this case, it's okay to judge a book by its cover. You'll see what others have said about the book. This may prompt you to make a more concerted effort once you turn to the pages within, or to abandon the book altogether—which could save you tons of time!
  - Scan the Internet for reader comments and reviews. Some online booksellers even offer lists of other books purchased by readers interested in the same area. Also, you can quickly find a description of many authors and books online.
  - Read the inside flaps of the book. The author usually writes this material. This is what the author wants you to know about the book and about him- or herself.
  - Read the foreword for more insight into what the book will teach, share, or explain to you. Many online booksellers provide PDF versions of the foreword, table of contents, and other key pages in the book. That way, even for the Internet shopper, you can know exactly what you'll be getting into with a particular book.
  - Read the table of contents. Some chapters may be worth reading immediately. There may be other chapters you determine that you can safely skip.
  - Read the introduction, which is usually written by the author; it also provides the reader with a stronger sense

of how the book came about and why the author wrote it. For a great example, see the first few pages of *The 60 Second Organizer*!

- Proceed to the chapters you have decided are worth some attention, and read the first two paragraphs to determine if you want to read the rest of the chapter. For those chapters where you don't want to continue, the first two paragraphs will at least give you a reasonable idea of what was covered.
- Go to the last page of each chapter and read either the last paragraph or any summary or list of highlights presented. These can be invaluable and, in some cases, can serve as a substitute for reading the entire chapter.
- Review any resource lists, reference lists, charts, or graphs that strike you as you are flipping through the book. Such features can be well worth the attention invested.
- In the last chapter, read the last two pages. Often, the author's major conclusions and observations are presented here, and this will save you reading at least the last chapter, possibly the last section of the book, or even the entire book. Finally, photocopy or print out the handful of key pages that have value to you.

Whenever you encounter a review of a book, an excerpt, a critique, or anything else that gives you the essence of what the book says, you are ahead of the game. Many libraries stock books and lectures on CD, and in most cases, these represent abridged versions of the longer tome. You can safely listen to a CD as you drive (an entirely different activity than talking on a cell phone—see tip #46). This is a palatable way to gain information, avoid eyestrain, and still arrive on time.

When you suspect that a periodical subscription is worth the money, but not worth your time, let your subscription expire with the last issue. If you don't miss the publication, then you've got it made. If you do miss reading it, the publication will take you back, with open arms, often at a reduced rate. If only all relationships worked that way. Perhaps you can gain the same information online, or visit the library periodically and peruse three or four issues of the same publication at high speed.

PART FIVE

Organize Online Activities, Meetings, and Travel

41 **Keep E-mail under Control** You send and receive e-mails all day long, and why not? E-mail is fast; it's transmitted nearly instantaneously after you push the send button. E-mail simply goes—which is why you receive so many every day. It's too convenient! You can send anything to anybody, and vice versa!

As you have too frequently witnessed, delivery of spam has risen dramatically, despite software filters and Internet Service Provider (ISP) crackdowns on offenders. Using unsecured, third-party servers, a spammer can target nearly every e-mail address found on the Net at practically no cost, since the ISP pays for the transmission. Some spammers send multimillions of messages of filth and smut with reckless abandon (and those are the nice guys). Some send schemes about moving multimillions of dollars out of Nigeria or East Hoshkosh. The spammers know that if only a tiny fraction of targets respond, the venture can be profitable.

Once you begin receiving a ton of spam along with regular e-mails, spending a brief time away from your computer allows a multitude of e-mails to pile up in your inbox, and that means you'll have scads of messages upon returning.

I advocate practicing triage for effective e-mail management. Triage is the method of quickly poring over a variety of items and allocating them based on what needs to be handled immediately, what can be handled later, and what can be ignored altogether. First, you want to eliminate the inane; this includes all forms of spam. After you eliminate the obvious junk, pick out which e-mails you can place in a holding folder, bin, or file. Some messages are worth saving but are not urgent. Some are from friends and loved ones, and you may want to read over their contents at leisure. Some will specify that a reply need not be immediate.

The final category is composed of those e-mail messages you receive that require immediate action. The number of messages that fall under this heading should be small. These e-mails are not necessarily urgent; they may merely prompt action. If you're able to respond to a request quickly and effortlessly, why waste time parking it? If the message is staring you in the face, and all you have to do is hit the reply button, type a few words, and send it, then do it!

In summary, for those e-mails that mandate your present, earnest, and speedy attention, do your best to handle them so that you can be mentally free of them.

42 **Manage Web Research and Protect Yourself** Thus far, Google has indexed at least 14.3 billion total Web pages. An estimated 71 billion static Web pages are publicly available on the Web. The Internet has all but taken over as our dominant form of entertainment, communication, and information resource, and more user-friendly applications are becoming available with each passing minute. As well, the Internet has become a major time drain.

On the heels of each problem related to Internet use comes application software and service-oriented sites that provide an antidote. Any specific program cited today will be quickly replaced, so instead, let's focus on two broad categories:

Bots: You can download one of these little buggers from Web sites such as *www.botspot.com* and it will search the Internet all day long, giving you the best possible prices and best deals for the products and services you're seeking. The most popular bots are used for shopping, but they can also be employed to ferret information on health, travel, and other bots!

Electronic clipping services: "Clipping" services, including *www .burrellesluce.com* and *www.cyberclipping.com,* offer you highly customized topic searches for a fee. Such sites can generate nearly everything that appears on the entire Web on any single day about a given company or topic. Alternatively, one good session employing a handful of the most popular search engines could be what you need to create a dossier packet for yourself of high-quality information and resources that could greatly accelerate your progress.

Back Up Thyself

Have you protected yourself by instituting a backup routine? What happens when your computer malfunctions or gets a virus? Does your system have the appropriate protection from online threats? Do you have your information backed up?

Total backups include all files and all directories on a given drive. Selective backups are simply that, selective, and include only named or highlighted files and directories. Modified backups include only those files that have changed in any way since the last backup was done. You never know when a natural or manmade disaster is going to destroy your computer or the information in it. If you're not sure how to make a backup of your computer system, contact the company that produced your software or the manufacturer of your computer. At such times, of course, a computer geek is a wonderful person to befriend.

There are numerous options on the market for backing up the information on your computer. From external hard drives, which often have more memory space than the original computer, to portable flash drives that plug into your USB port, you can safely protect your computer files. There are many online backup providers that—for free or a small fee—allot a reserved amount of space to back up files. In a pinch, you can even use an iPod or Zune to back up files. The possibilities are plentiful and there's no reason to lose your important electronic information!

43 **Conduct More Productive Meetings—Really!** Now, on to face-to-face communications. Do you regard meetings as a massively efficient way to completely suck the time and energy out of day? Or is that an understatement? Some people have such great dislike for meetings that they feel stressed and anxious the moment they learn they have to attend one, let alone conduct one. Despite the fact that many managers dislike calling meetings, and staff often dread attending them, studies show that people today are spending more time in face-to-face and virtual meetings, and on a greater variety of topics with a variety of objectives, than ever before.

Former Secretary of State Dr. Henry Kissinger once said that there was no purpose in having a meeting unless the desired outcomes were known in advance. The typical meeting is arranged by one person to convey information to many people. Ideally, the attendees will reflect upon what they heard, generate wonderful ideas, and take bold, decisive action to the delight of the meeting chair. What usually occurs is a lot of thumb twiddling, text-messaging under the table, pencil tapping, and daydreaming.

In face-to-face encounters, people shuffle into the meeting room and listen dully to some new stuff that they have to do or learn or take back to others. They doodle, guzzle coffee, and manage to fall asleep. Most of what they hear is quickly forgotten. Scratching your nails across a chalkboard will only get their attention long enough for them to cringe at the noise. Whatever they're supposed to do is rarely done on time or in the way the meeting manager had hoped for. There's got to be a better way—and, just for you, there is.

A far more effective and organized way to conduct a meeting, even for virtual meetings, is to elicit the participation of those who will be a part of the meeting, long before it even starts. Yes, you read it correctly. It would only take two to four minutes per attendee for you to:

- Speak with people who will be attending the meeting
- Prep them for what will be discussed during the meeting
- Hear their views about what they're going to get out of the meeting
- Treat them as partners, not subjects

If your group meets on an ongoing basis, ask participants questions beforehand, such as:

- What methods have worked well for you in any previous meetings?
- How can we proceed in a manner that involves everyone?
- What would you like to get out of this meeting?

The above may sound like extra work. Consider, however, that meetings aren't held for the purpose of simply gathering a bunch of people; they're held presumably to accomplish some worthwhile objective. If discussing meeting objectives with participants will greatly accelerate progress, why wouldn't you want to do this? The meeting is likely to take less time, which will result in greater participation and, ideally, greater advancement toward the desired objective. Moreover, participants actually report high enthusiasm for this process. It makes them feel important; they see that their input matters. They may anticipate the meeting with a new perspective, since they know that "this one" is going to be different. They might even have fun!

Some managers dread the thought of having to preinterview meeting participants. "Gosh, talk to each person one at a time!

How overwhelming." Yet, the process doesn't have to be strenuous if it's carried out in an organized fashion. Preinterviewing attendees gives you a leg up on exactly how to proceed:

1. You design a custom agenda that focuses on topics identified as important to the entire group.
2. You arrange the topics in an order conducive to achieving the group's overall objectives.
3. You circulate the agenda in advance so that participants come armed with ideas on how and when they can best contribute.

As a result, the meeting is far more likely to stay on course, end on time, and encourage participants to be more enthusiastic for the next meeting! And they regard you as an organized, competent manager. As you'll see with the very next meeting, when participants have a vested interest in the content of a meeting, they attend on time and are ready from the start. When they receive an agenda in advance that specifies the precise starting time, they have yet another indicator of the importance of being there.

As a meeting manager, it behooves you to steadfastly start meetings on time so that stragglers will realize that they are late and that the others arrived as scheduled. Organized managers start meetings on time!

In his book *Breakthrough Business Meetings*, Robert Levasseur suggests that at the start of any meeting, "participants reach a common understanding of what they're going to do and how they're going to do it." Hence, everyone needs to be ready from the get-go. Levasseur says that this normally consumes 10 percent of the meeting time, so if you're going to be in a meeting for thirty minutes, you only need three minutes or so to deal with some basic issues, such as the following.

- The main purpose of the meeting
- The participants' desired outcomes
- The actual agenda itself
- The key meeting roles, which for smaller groups is understood at the outset

After you make it clear that a strict start time is the norm, some individuals may still arrive tardy to meetings. This is true both for face-to-face meetings and for virtual meetings. How rude! There are several techniques, which work to varying degrees of effectiveness, to encourage promptness:

- In some organizations, tardy people have to apologize to the group. Then it becomes their responsibility afterward to catch up with the group for the parts they missed. Never backtrack for late arrivals; it will only cause everyone to stop and wait while the guilty party receives a personalized briefing.
- In some organizations, plum assignments are handed out in the first few minutes so that tardy people are left with the least desirable tasks. This is a great incentive for arriving early. In certain organizations, and this is not my preference, the tardy are the subject of early discussion. In other words, they are the target of gossip, innuendoes, and jokes. You could always use the old "sit in the corner with a dunce hat" approach if all else fails.
- In some organizations, for face-to-face meetings, the room doors are locked (only for the bold!). Anyone who tries to enter late has to knock on the door. Depending on how charitable you're feeling, the knocks may or may not be answered on the first round. Tardy attendees then sheepishly take their seats.

In my first job, if you were late for a meeting, you had to throw a dollar into the kitty for every minute you were late. Sure as heck, nobody ever walked in more than five minutes late. I have no idea what they used the money for!

You may quickly catch on that none of these subtle coercions are as effective as preinterviewing participants, circulating an agenda, and demonstrating on a repeated basis that the meetings start promptly as scheduled.

44 **Sustain Successful Meetings Without Stopping** When participants know in advance that a particular item on the docket will be allotted five minutes, most people do their best to honor that time frame. Hence, a strong, organized agenda in the best possible sequence, and estimated time frames for each agenda item is the winning formula for keeping meetings on track.

You follow the agenda, eliciting the input of others as needed. You encourage attendees to participate. As each agenda item is discussed, ask participants to keep in mind the following questions: What is the specific issue being discussed? What does the group want to accomplish in discussing the item? What action needs to be taken to handle the issue?

When the necessary action is identified, key questions include: Who will act? What type of resources does he or she require? When will the issue be resolved? When will the group discuss the results? Upon successful conclusion of these questions, the group then moves on to the next issue.

Not all issues require proceeding through every question. Sometimes an agenda item merely represents an announcement or a report to the group that doesn't require any feedback or discussion. Sometimes the issue at hand represents an executive briefing, because the matter has already been resolved. On occasion, unnecessary discussion ensues, and an item ends up requiring twice as much time as originally allotted. Often, however, participants make up for the overflow in one area by being briefer in other areas.

When you are addressing a group whose participants have been preinterviewed and an agenda has been circulated in advance, there are a variety of techniques you can use to keep the meeting organized and on track. Each technique will vary in effectiveness, depending on the purpose of your group, how often it meets, and your group's history. Consider some of the following suggestions for your meetings:

- Require participants to keep their remarks within an allotted time frame. Some groups keep a timer in plain view of all participants to encourage them to keep their comments brief. Others meet in a room with a wall clock in view. For virtual meetings conducted over the Web, various clocks and timers abound.
- Have the meeting manager announce who will be speaking next and how many minutes have been allocated for the topic on the agenda.
- Ask participants to circulate summaries of their comments, charts, or exhibits in advance that illustrate the points they wish to make. For virtual meetings, all such items can be circulated in advance via e-mail. Then, have them offer brief commentary to highlight the information in distributed materials.

When you preassign times to each issue, participants may actually seek to stay within those time frames! When you elicit time frames from the participants in advance, it behooves them to stay on track. If someone admits in advance that only three minutes are needed for a particular issue, then that individual is less likely to run on and on and on. . . . Get to the point, already! Here are other ideas to keep meetings organized and on course:

- Ask participants in face-to-face meetings to stand when they speak. This tends to limit the time that they speak, because most people prefer to stay seated. Also, much time will be saved if people merely stand at their chairs and speak instead of ambling to the front of the room.
- Encourage meeting participants to arrive early and stay late. This is applicable in virtual meetings, too. Then they are more likely to get down to business during the meeting because they have time to banter and joke around both before and after the meeting (as opposed to during the meeting).
- Request that those who can't be in attendance submit what they would have said in a concise paragraph or two to be read by someone in attendance.

The organized meeting manager knows the importance of building some slack into all meetings. For example, a manager may allocate five minutes for a topic that he or she will personally be covering, knowing that it will actually require about three minutes. Hence, several minutes can be saved here and there. So, even if somebody goes over the allotted time frame, the meeting still stays on track and ends on time. What a world.

For virtual meetings, where some or all of the meeting participants are in remote locations and dialing in, logging on, tuning in, or what have you, your job as host, chair, MC, moderator, or presenter can be a bit more challenging. For virtual meetings without video, such as conference calls or Webinars, use your voice to best advantage. Vary your tone, rate, and inflection. Be lively, be interesting, or be gone.

If any type of real-time video is employed, such a Webcams or virtual meeting projectors, above all use your face as a medium for gestures. If you can raise an eyebrow, grimace, act surprised, or look excited it's all to the good, because the audience only has you to go on, and they need visual cues.

In general, vary your rate of speech and amplitude. Sometimes, lean in toward the camera and speak softly. Other times, say something loud, or twice, for emphasis. Don't be afraid to pause, especially if you've just said something you'd like the participants to reflect upon. A pause, offered correctly, can be a moment of high drama.

If you're using visuals and graphics, have them ready in advance and in sequence. This is no time to be bumbling around. If your meeting contains a mixed live and long-distance audience, draw your energy from the people before you, but from time to time give your attention to the participants out there in the great beyond. You might say "for those listening from afar . . ." or something of that nature. Stay confident while you're conducting the show. After all, you are the leader, aren't you?

45 **Congregate to Accomplish** Some groups meet with an accountant, an attorney, or another advisor in attendance as a method of keeping the meeting on track and headed toward the desired objectives. International Toastmaster meetings, for example, include a parliamentarian who routinely advises the group as to when they have strayed from established protocol. Some groups choose to have one person serve as timer. Also, you or some other designated attendee may decide when a matter is best handled by a smaller group, such as a task force or selected team.

For those items on the agenda that have a corresponding objective, you have the responsibility to track the progress. What else needs to be accomplished, and by when, to meet the overall objective? As with any goal or objective (see tip #19), they need to be:

- Written down
- Quantified
- Assigned specific time frames

The quickest way to lose the participants in face-to-face meetings, other than being an interminable, crashing bore, is to conduct your meeting in a room where the temperature is too high, or where ventilation is poor. That, coupled with a dark meeting room, encourages people to fall asleep. It's a biological phenomenon—as soon as it's dark, the brain receives the message that it's time to doze off. A warm, stuffy room only aids the process. They'll be snoring in no time—you might even have a few droolers.

You always want to meet in a well-lit room with excellent ventilation. If you have a choice between having a room slightly too warm or slightly too cool, opt for cool. A cool room will keep participants fresh and alert. The discomfort may prompt attendees to complain, and a little frostbite might result, but at least no one will go to sleep. If participants need to take written notes or work from laptop computers, make sure there are flat surfaces on which they can work. Pens, pads, cold water, and possibly tea or coffee should also be available. In some groups, the secretary or transcriber takes notes on everything that is being said. Other groups use the far more efficient digital recorder and have the notes transcribed afterward.

For virtual meetings, when people are connected by phone, PC, screen, projected image, or other emerging virtual reality technologies, it's vital to keep the meeting moving at a brisk pace, constantly involve all participants, and solicit feedback. Otherwise, it's relatively easy for remote participants to drift off, multitask, or simply "play along."

Whatever your recording method happens to be, set up and check out recorders, pocket dictators, projectors, slides, chalkboards, whiteboards, Webcams and all other equipment far before the meeting begins. If you'll be giving a slide presentation, be sure that you have the file backed up on multiple mediums, in case there is some technical difficulty, such as if your laptop isn't compatible with the projection system in the room. Also check for replacement batteries, light bulbs, extension cords, whips (in case someone dozes off), and all supporting equipment in advance.

If your meeting lasts longer than thirty minutes, it could be useful to schedule breaks some time in the middle, so as not to lose the attention of your participants. You may also lose their attention simply because attention spans in this day and age are only so long. Hmm . . . it's a good thing this is a short book!

Here are some other room organizing techniques for conducting face-to-face meetings:

- Meet in a room where participants won't be disturbed by ringing phones, people knocking on the door, and other intrusions. You want to achieve a meeting of the minds and accomplish great things; distractions do not help.
- Meet where there is wall-to-wall carpeting and walls adorned with pictures, posters, and the like to help absorb sounds and offer a richer texture to the voices being heard. Contrast this environment with a meeting held in a room with a tile floor, cold metal chairs, and blank, thin walls. Participants can't wait for the meeting to be over when the

meeting room feels like a holding cell, no matter what's being discussed.

- Meet where the seats are comfortable and supportive. However, overly comfortable seats may encourage people to nod off. Ideally, everyone's seat would be the same, with none higher or lower than any other.

Maintain a supportive atmosphere for all participants; otherwise, comments come off as edicts (i.e., "I say, you do"). Edicts don't encourage people to attend meetings in the future, even when something vital and interesting is being presented.

Serve as a facilitator. When you offer positive guidance, you elicit the best of responses from participants, encouraging them to cooperate with one another and function as a team. In the smallest of groups, as well as in larger gatherings, the diverse backgrounds and personalities of participants ensure that there will be clashes on occasion. Help keep the disruption to a minimum.

Many managers, in an erroneous attempt to "save time," don't bother to gather any feedback from participants following a meeting. They figure that their own observations were plenty, so why bother taking the time to consult with others? Remember, there is no "I" in "team" (although by rearranging the letters there is a "me". . .). Organized and effective meeting managers have the courage to engage in meeting follow-up. They speak with participants afterward to learn if participants thought the meeting was effective, what could be added, what could be dropped, and how it could be improved.

The manager then takes these suggestions back, ruminates on them, and actually incorporates into the next meeting those that would make a significant contribution. If meeting participants are assigned to reach an objective, they realize the meeting manager can facilitate that by having more effective meetings. Ultimately, listening to feedback from participants is a time saver for the manager.

46 **Organize for the Drive** In every metropolitan and suburban area throughout the United States, and increasingly in traffic throughout the world, commuting has become drudgery. You crawl along bumper to bumper, inhaling the fumes of the thousands of cars on a superhighway that effectively operates like a slow-moving parking lot.

When you're driving a car, even at a snail's pace, your principal activity is driving. A study published by the *New England Journal of Medicine* showed that driving while speaking on a cell phone makes you four times as likely to get into an accident and eleven times as likely to be killed while driving. It's as dangerous as driving drunk. Why? You can only focus your sharp attention in one direction.

If you're at a traffic light or sitting in slowly moving traffic, it is still hazardous to speak on a cell phone, even a hands-free cell phone. Pull off to the side of the road if you can't function without making a call. Gee, how did motorists manage for the first 100 years? Conversely, listening to the radio or to a CD, or speaking with someone in the passenger seat, does not pose the same risk. Your sharp attention can continue to be on the road even as you tune in to the radio, a CD, or the passenger in the seat next to you. This is because your driving takes precedence. You can sing your heart out and be safe at the same time. This is not the case with the use of the cell phone—concentrating on the conversation with someone at a distance and driving compete with one another.

Palatable Partners
If you are going to ride with others to work as part of a carpool or vanpool, choose people you like to talk to. Surprisingly, you may

have more lively conversations with someone who does not work with you, and you will both benefit from the conversation.

Close your windows for a quieter ride and better control of your environment. If you decide to listen to something, play an invigorating or inspiring CD. Investigate services such as recorded books. Visit your library and find lectures, plays, and essays on audio. Or, turn on some classical music: The rhythms and composition have been shown to promote healing and well-being, unlike other forms of music, which can have a disconcerting effect.

Now, to the matter of organizing your vehicle—keeping your car in top running condition is the major prerequisite to successful driving. You only have to break down once in a strange location to experience how unproductive your day can become. Take your car in for a tune-up on a regular basis, as the manufacturer recommends. Bring it in any time you even suspect that something is not operating as it ought to be. Waiting until the brakes no longer stop your car is probably not the safest way to maintain your vehicle.

A major key to personal effectiveness while commuting is to use that time for reflection. Instead of automatically flipping on the radio, you can organize your thoughts en route to your various destinations. Consider what's on your agenda for the morning, what you'll be doing, whom you will be meeting, and then see yourself successfully handling it all. Contemplate eating your lunch, coming back from lunch, having appointments, taking care of projects, meeting with others, or other imminent activities.

Navigate Errands While Commuting

Here is a masterstroke of organizing effectiveness: Instead of letting your errands stack up for the weekends, designate one night per week as "errand night." Make, for example, Tuesday the night on which you will handle errands on the way back from work.

Prepare for multiple stops. You may wish to make a brief list of your errands and affix it to your dashboard. Keep a file folder, envelope, or pouch handy for assembling the various coupons, sales slips, and so forth that you will be dispensing and collecting. If you can, keep the passenger side of your car clear so that it serves as your command center on wheels. This will also make your passengers happy that their laps don't become home to everything you throw in your seat.

If you encounter traffic backups and long lines, or other undue delays while making your errand run, fold up the tent and head home. What's the use of trying to force your way through the crowds? You can get your stress in other ways. You always have the option of handling errands on another night, still preserving your weekends, and accomplishing everything in less time and with less hassle.

Buy in multiples so you don't have to return to various stores as often. When it is practical, go online and find vendors who pick up and deliver (see tip #57). Have vendors come to you.

Rather than buying stamps at the post office, order them by mail. Rather than dropping off deposits at the bank, mail them in. Every time that you don't have to get into your car to accomplish something, you save time, preserve your vehicle, and preserve your sanity, not to mention saving money from astronomical gas prices. As more of what you need to do is accessible via catalogs and the Internet, you may find that a few hours a week is more than enough time to handle the errands for which you need to be physically present.

47 **Commute Astutely** Do you claw your way into work, mile by mile? To avoid the masses in the morning and afternoon, depart when everyone else isn't. If you can head out on the road an hour or an hour and a half earlier than everyone else, or for that matter, an hour or an hour and a half later, you're likely to have smoother sailing.

Consider getting up at your normal time, working for an hour and a half at home, and then departing for the office. Maybe you can leave work early in the afternoon, arrive home without fighting a lot of traffic, and then continue with your work at home. Perhaps you prefer to leave after everyone else does at the end of the day. To keep yourself on track, put a few key items in your car in advance.

Attach an extra set of car keys someplace under the bumper in one of those magnetic hide-a-key compartments. Also, have spare house keys hidden in your car, as you would have spare car keys somewhere in your house. Getting locked out is not productive. Calling somebody to open your car is a waste of time and money, and it's just plain annoying for all parties involved. Hide a roll of dimes and quarters in your car to use for parking meters and vending machines. Be sure to have a car charger for your cell phone, in case your phone battery dies. You never know when you might have an emergency. Also, put a backup briefcase or folder in your trunk with stamps, envelopes, a pen, paper, a calculator, and perhaps important phone numbers.

What else is worth storing in the car? You may store a gym bag with socks, extra underwear, a toothbrush, tissues, flashlight, sunglasses, credit cards, maps of the area, library cards, first-aid kit, umbrella, a raincoat, a hat, and some gloves, among other things.

It's also a good idea to keep a blanket in your car in case you are stranded somewhere cold. Some people have been known to store rolls of toilet paper in their cars. Hey, if you gotta go, you gotta go. When you become acutely aware of the cost of being locked out of your car, delayed, or stuck in the city unprepared, you'll get prepared.

If you're not a member of one of the national auto clubs, such as AAA (*www.aaa.com*), the National Auto Club (*www.national autoclub.com*), or the Better World Club (*www.betterworldclub.com*), or one of the auto industry–derived clubs such as the GM Motor Club, the Amoco Motor Club, BP Motor Club, or Chevron Motor Club, consider the advantages of joining. Even if your car needs a jump-start or tow only once per year, the annual cost of membership will pay for itself. Having this kind of security is priceless. By dialing an 800 number, you can have a top-flight garage with a qualified towing specialist on the scene usually in forty-five minutes or less almost wherever you are.

Once a week, if you can, telecommute—avoid going into the office at all. Get wired to your office by fax, Internet, and telephone if you're not already. If you stay home even one Wednesday every other week, you're far more productive in handling the kinds of tasks that are hard to tackle in a hectic office. Plus, you can wear your pajamas all day.

48 **Ride Public Transportation with a Purpose** If you are among the less than 10 percent of the working population who commute to work via public transportation, my figurative hat is off to you. Though cities have designed vast subway and bus systems, the majority of commuters still get to work by automobile. There are many ways to be productive while on a bus, subway, train, or in a van. You already know most of them, so we will be brief here.

To tune out surrounding noise on a mass transit system, use a portable CD or MP3 player. Surely you've seen all those people walking around with the telltale white headphones. Choose what you want to hear, but make sure that it's uplifting, informative, and generally supports how you want to be and feel in life. If you opt to read the newspaper, that's fine. If you're reading this book right now on the train, more power to you! Do me a favor and tell the person sitting next to you how helpful and inspiring it is.

If you travel with a laptop or notebook computer, you probably already have your routine down pat. Depending on the brightness of your screen, you may wish to sit on the nonsunny side of the vehicle. Supply yourself with plenty of recharged batteries for the ride.

Do not house your expensive computer in a traditional carrying case; these are ready-made targets for thieves. Instead, carry expensive equipment in a satchel, a rather worn briefcase, or some other ratty carrying case that looks like it would be used to house anything but a computer.

The lighter you travel, the more adept you will be at getting on and off the bus, subway, train, or other vehicle. If you have been commuting for any length of time, you know how long the ride will take, so you can plan your work accordingly. I've seen many adept professionals practice what I call vest pocket management. They are able to pull out a pad or pen, business cards, sticky notes, an electronic organizer, a handheld calendar, a pocket dictator, or a variety of other work-related tools from their vest pockets. They can start working at the drop of a hat and pack up as quickly.

If you read voraciously during your time on public transportation, stay lean and mean. When plowing through magazines, quickly extract those articles that represent something important and urgent, or at least important, and recycle the rest of the magazine. Your goal while traveling is to always have less at the end of your trip to carry.

Retain the smallest volume of paper that serves your purposes. For example, if you only need a Web site address, a phone number, or a key bit of information, don't save pages and pages from an article. Instead, save the one key page that contains the information you need.

The availability of handheld scanners makes it possible to scan in one line of text at a time, copying only the information that you need, and as a result carry exceedingly little paper. Or, if you travel with a pocket dictator, you can record the key phrases, phone numbers, and other tidbits of information you wish to retain. Later you can transcribe your recording, or better yet, have someone else transcribe it, and transfer the information to your hard drive.

If you travel with a cell phone or a pocket dictator, be respectful of other passengers. Turn away from the open area, modulate your voice, and keep your conversations as short as possible. As the wall poster says on the mainline trains out of Philadelphia, use your "inside voice." You may be taking care of all kinds of business with your sleek little phone, but to others nearby, you are a noisy offender. Most people simply have no interest in knowing what time your meeting is and who will be there.

Checking for voice mail messages, e-mail, and other correspondence can, of course, all be easily handled while in transit. But don't whip yourself into a frenzy over the gathering of these messages. They'll still be there when you arrive at your destination.

49 **Pack Practically** With the increase in passengers, more restrictive airline configuration, and heightened and tightened security, airline travel has become a pain. The key to staying organized and productive before, during, and after flying is to stay light and take care of as many things as you can in advance.

- Pack the night before and pack as light as you can.
- When practical, mail things ahead rather than pack them.

- Use the least number of toiletries and less-than-3-ounce sizes.
- Allow for extra time for every facet of air travel (hey, that's reality).
- Use rolling luggage to avoid having to lift your heavy bag.

Most airlines will accept carry-on luggage of 22 inches by 14 inches by 9 inches. Thus, you can roll your luggage onto the plane and never have to check your bag, saving a good fifteen to twenty minutes prior to your departure, and upon arrival at your destination. If you have to pack a second bag, use something that fits on the top of your rolling cart luggage; essentially, you are not lifting either bag, but rolling them both. An airport is not the place to work on your biceps.

Use self-service check-in any time you can. If you have the opportunity to attain frequent passenger status, use it to speed through the baggage check! Long lines are a drag, and your mission is to bypass as many as you can.

Regardless, be prepared to encounter the security checkpoint and avoid becoming your line's bottleneck. In other words, don't simply stand in line until it's your turn, then rush to pull out your passport and toiletries and take off your shoes and jewelry. Prepare before your stroll through the metal detector. Don't be the one holding up the line! Have your 3-ounce bottles of shampoo, moisturizer, toothpaste, and the like in a plastic bag and at the ready. And don't be that guy—the one who argues with the security official when he or she doesn't let you take something on the plane. Find out beforehand. Travel guidelines for domestic and overseas travelers can be found on the Transportation Security Administration's Web site, *www.tsa.gov*.

If you're going on a lengthy trip with many stops, rather than packing clothes for each day, bring enough clothing for half the trip plus one day. Hence, if you are traveling for nine days, pack five days' worth of clothing. No one will judge you for wearing the same pair of jeans twice in a row. If you are traveling for ten days, take six days' worth of clothing. Then, as you approach the halfway point of your trip, get everything cleaned while on the road. Taking advantage of laundry and valet services costs a little money, but you're better off shelling out a little money here and there than toting around a bulky bag of heavy and increasingly dirty clothing.

Keep your briefcase packed lightly and efficiently. Carry a few Priority Mail packages with you so that as you collect documents and information during your travels you can mail them back to yourself rather than continuing to carry them. The Priority Mail package is relatively inexpensive. Bring address labels for both your destination and your home base. This saves you from writing your name and address over and over.

Don't pack anything that you know your hotel or host destination already supplies. You can always call in advance to get the list of what is offered. It can be a great boon if you don't have to pack a bathrobe, an alarm clock, a hairdryer, and other overnight necessities. Save the little soaps and other toiletries the hotel offers. The little weight and volume is ideal for subsequent trips, they come in handy, and some just smell so good.

50 **Travel Right for Your Flight** If you enjoy long lines and major grief, buy tickets at the airline ticket counter the day of your departure. If you do, you are likely to receive the worst seats at the highest price. Nice deal, eh? Poor seating will negatively impact your productivity and use of time while onboard. You want to buy your tickets in advance so that you can get a bulkhead, a wing row, or an aisle seat. Each of these offers more room than the middle seat or the window location.

Always bring a water bottle with you that you can fill up after the security checkpoint so that you do not have to wait for flight attendants to come around to quench your thirst. A few sips here and there can make all the difference between maintaining high energy and high productivity, and being sluggish, dehydrated, and not able to get quality work completed.

Bring your own snacks. Yes, pack your own food and don't scowl! What do you pack? You can bring carrots, cucumbers, apples, bananas, sunflower seeds, peanuts, and anything else that is healthy and will give you an energy boost. Avoid buying candy, cupcakes, and other heavily sugared or salted items, such as pretzels, prepackaged cheese and crackers, and other widely commercially available snack foods that offer nothing more than dead carbohydrates. Empty carbs are the enemy! These will drain you of energy, leave your body nutrient-starved, and cause you to operate with far less efficiency than is otherwise possible.

Sitting in an airplane seat for hours on end is confining. Avoid heavy clothing, tight shoes, restrictive belts, and anything else that reduces respiration, ventilation, and circulation. If you're meeting a client as soon as you land at your destination, you may have to sacrifice wearing what you want by wearing a suit or dressy attire. Otherwise, wear loose and comfortable clothing. You want to be able to move around freely in your awkwardly small seat and enjoy the flight. You don't have to look glamorous all the time.

If you are flying midday when the sun's ultraviolet rays are more pronounced, carry sunglasses with you. Also use the airline overhead lighting and lower your window cover. Your eyes won't get nearly as fatigued. In our ultramobile society, the chances are increasing that you will be spending time in a moving vehicle. By making adequate preparations in advance, you maximize your potential for being at your best while in motion and afterward.

PART SIX

Making Your Home Your Castle

51 **Reclaim Your Spaces** In this last section of the book, we'll focus on getting organized in your personal life since it so clearly supports your efforts in your professional life. When you think about it, the activities required to keep a den or car organized are basically no different than the activities that you already undertake at the places where you have no difficulty keeping organized! Simply apply the best of what you are doing in one place or space to another and you'll find that staying organized is not so tough.

The more organized you are at home, at work, and in other places in your life, the greater the probability that you will have more focus, energy, and direction when you head into work. You will certainly be more efficient, and perhaps have greater peace of mind.

To ensure that your home environment enhances your sense of control, don't allow ad hoc outposts to build up. Many career professionals today have some type of home office. In any event, adopt supportive docking and unloading techniques. Always bring mail, office work you've brought home, tax receipts, and newly purchased items (including warranties and tags) to their final destinations or to your "administrative outpost" for processing and integration into your organization system. The more often you're able to keep the surfaces, such as the dining room table, your desk, and small tables clear, the greater your ability to manage the flow of items in your life, deal with them capably, and move on. The kitchen table is not a landfill! Don't dump everything on it.

Remaining organized starts when you come in the door. Avoid leaving things at inappropriate outposts. Take items to their end destinations when you get home, or shortly thereafter. If an item belongs in the den, take it to the den. If it belongs in the closet, go to the closet.

When you fail to take items to their end destinations, you create double and triple the work for yourself. Do you want to do that to yourself? Maybe to someone else, but certainly not to yourself. The piling up of little, unfinished chores can make you feel overwhelmed. Upon returning from travel, immediately unpack your bags, put clothes in the closet or washer, and take all paperwork to your desk.

If you keep a small cabinet or table by the door, use it only for what is leaving your home, never for what is entering. What enters goes directly to its final resting place. What exits departs soon. The process of moving stuff out should be continual, just like at work.

If mornings are a mad rush for you, lighten your load by reducing the number of items you have to round up and things you have to do. Visit your car the night before and stock it as fully as possible with the items you or your children need for the next day. This includes office files, books, gym clothes, and lunch bags—whatever doesn't spoil.

At home, if your closets are jam-packed with stuff you have stowed over the years, it's time to engage in spring cleaning, whether spring is here or not. If you can't bear to part with all the stuff you've crammed in there, at least separate it by the seasons.

I promise you won't need your fur coat when the temperature hits 90 degrees. As spring approaches, box up all the winter items and put them in an out-of-the-way part of the house. Perhaps they can go into the attic, the basement, or some infrequently used room. It should take you sixty minutes or less for each closet. Once each closet is organized, it is set for at least a season. That's three whole months before you have to do this again!

As you proceed through your house reclaiming spaces, you'll find the payoff spills over into your career. The twenty-first-century man or woman is simply inundated with too many items competing for time and attention, whether it is at work, at home, or in between. Cramming an unreasonable number of activities into a given unit of time perceptually tends to make that time speed by. Likewise, cramming too many items into a physical space tends to make you feel out of control. You can only hide so much under your bed.

By banishing enemy outposts and reclaiming your spaces, you can find things faster and easier, save time, depart more easily in the morning, and stow things more easily at the end of the day.

52 **Commit to a Cleaning Day** Many career professionals devote some part of Friday afternoon to "office housekeeping" if they don't already have some pressing assignment or deadline. Actually, Friday afternoon is a stupendous time to refile and straighten up the desk and surrounding areas. Why Friday? For many people there is more noise in the office on that day than on any other. Also, some people have a hard time staying focused as the last few hours of the work week wind down. Happy hour is oh so close!

If others in your office adopt the habit of straightening up on Fridays, then it's all the more convenient for you to do so as well. You'll be part of the office milieu. Then you can leave for the weekend with a sense of control over your professional environment.

Regardless of the day and the time you choose, develop an organizing maintenance routine. You'll find that those onerous, recurring, organizing-related tasks are not so big and, all told, not so bad.

As a corollary, when it comes to putting one's home in order, some people find the work week to be too hectic, so they wait until Friday evening or Saturday morning. Rhonda, for example, is too exhausted during the week as well as on Friday evening to even entertain the idea of putting her house in order. After a good night's rest on Friday, however, she is revived and ready to go.

She starts the wash soon after rising and then vacuums the house as the washing machine is going through its cycles. When the wash cycle is finished, she puts the clothes in the dryer and then begins working in the kitchen, handling any dirty dishes and silverware, cleaning the sink, and sweeping the floor. By the time it becomes necessary to take the clothes out of the dryer and fold them, she is approaching the finish line of her Saturday-morning ritual.

As Rhonda distributes items to the linen closet, bedroom drawers, and closets, she straightens up each of these rooms quickly. Then she finishes cleaning the two bathrooms in her home. In ninety minutes or thereabouts, presto! Her work is done. Thereafter, only a few maintenance activities are necessary during the rest of Saturday and Sunday, and with enough nagging, she can get her husband to do those. In any event, she does her best to hold the line during the week.

Invariably, by next Friday the house is a mess again. Not to worry. Rhonda does not stress out, because she maintains a regular day and time when she puts things in order. If she's away one Saturday morning or some circumstance arises, she temporarily rearranges her schedule and maintains order nonetheless.

In your own situation at work or at home, pick a regular day and time, like Rhonda, and you too can maintain order. You might even be the first on your block.

53 **Strategize to Organize** Train yourself to think strategically when approaching your spaces at home just as you've now learned to do at work. For example, consider your linen closet.

The linen closet is a restricted space for storage of your linens and towels. Organize them in such a way that all you have to do is open the door and, behold, the items that you need are at your fingertips. No more blankets and oversized towels tumbling down on you as soon as you open the door!

To maintain order, store towels of the same size together. Avoid stowing frequently used items on high shelves. If towels and washcloths will be retrieved from the linen closet every day or every other day, it makes sense to have them be accessible to everyone who needs them, including shorter people and small children. There's no need to pull out the grappling hooks just to take a shower.

Your linen closet can contain a variety of other things besides linens, towels, and washcloths. This includes anything that is not easily stored within the bathroom. You don't want your linen closet overflowing with bathroom supplies; however, you can make it complement your bathroom, housing those items for which there is no additional room in the bathroom. For example:

- Stow some of the larger items that cannot be stored easily in the bathroom, such as a hair dryer or other electrical devices, in the linen closet.
- Employ small boxes to keep a variety of supplies neatly organized. These items could include extra soap, shampoo, toothpaste, and various personal hygiene items.
- Use the height of shelves to determine what goes where. For example, if you have small children and you want them to be able to reach washcloths, these would go on lower shelves. Your linen closet is not a jungle gym. There should be no climbing involved. Alternatively, if there are items that children should not be touching, like cleaning supplies, for example, these would go on the highest shelves.

Some people use the far reaches of the linen closet to store extra supplies, while they stack their towels, washcloths, bed sheets, or pillowcases closer to the front of each shelf. When you open the linen closet, you should only see fabric items. It may seem like a small point, but sometimes visually arranging the closet is as helpful as anything else you can do to maintain the feeling of being in control. When you strategically approach your linen closet or any other of your vital spaces, you have a better chance of devising an orderly system that will serve you well.

Apply strategic thinking to other areas of your home. If you can't see the floor of your closet, organize your shoes. You can buy ready-built shoe caddies at most discount stores or simply use a shoe bag. If you get a shoe bag you can hang it on the wall in your closet or on the back of the door. Shoe bags made of a mesh material are particularly useful because you can see which shoes are in which compartment, and you don't have to bend over to find them. You can even get creative on this one; for example, use old wine racks to hold your shoes. Visit a store such as Bed, Bath & Beyond, Linens-n-Things, Hold Your Own, or any of the other home center stores dotting the horizon and you'll encounter a variety of "shoe organizing" systems. Some of these can be quite complex, so you'll need to come prepared with closet measurements, a total shoe count, and a structural engineer. Take measurements of your closets so that you can determine which of these devices might comfortably fit within the space that you have and work well for your shoe fetish. One of the grandest shoe-organizing techniques is giving away those that you don't wear anymore.

Undoubtedly, you have community groups that would gladly accept donations of shoes, including Goodwill, the Salvation Army, and if you belong to one, your own church. Be honest with yourself in deciding which shoes you will actually wear and which ones can safely be given away. Otherwise, the seldom-worn shoes will populate your closet for the rest of your days. Some shoes you might be more than happy to be rid of, like those hot pink pumps with the purple bows you were forced to wear in your sister's wedding. Plus, this is a good excuse; she can't get too angry with a charitable donation. You will feel good about giving away the excess shoes (especially if they're sorry-looking), and if the spirit moves you, you will have more room available for acquiring new shoes! At last, an honorable reason to go shoe shopping!

54 **Employ the Replacement Principle** As you begin regaining some order in your home life, here is an insightful and practical way to keep accumulations from engulfing you: Employ the replacement principle. When you acquire something new, something else has to go. The following chart offers examples of nonreplacement policies contrasted with replacement policies. (Note: This policy does not work well for replacing children—you can't just give them back, you know.)

Nonreplacement Policies	Replacement Policies
Your child's collection of DVDs grows beyond fifty as you acquire the classics as well as latest hits.	You decide with your child in advance on a total number of DVDs he or she can have. Each new one means replacing an old one.
Your file cabinet keeps growing until you need to buy another.	Your files stay the same size, because for each item you add, you discard one.
Old equipment can be found in closets and storage bins. You hang on to it thinking it's going to have future value.	When you buy new equipment, you donate older equipment to a charitable organization and get a tax deduction.
You've collected books since college and now have overflowing shelves with no hope of reading most of what you've collected.	You retain only books of continuing or sentimental value. You quickly scan or copy the pages that are most important to you, and give the books away.

Nonreplacement Policies	Replacement Policies
Although you have a 284GB hard disk, you are considering getting more disk space.	You don't need any additional hard disk space, because at least monthly, you routinely prune your disk of outdated files.
You have a collection of annual reports, 401(k) statements, and the like from investment houses, most of which you haven't read.	When you receive an annual report from an investment firm, you quickly replace what they sent you last year with the new one.
Your clothes drawers and closets are overfilled, mostly with items you haven't worn in years.	There is more than sufficient space to house the clothes that you actually use, because you give the rest to charities.
You have a trailer load of brochures and memorabilia from your last trip, and many previous trips as well.	You have a few choice mementos from your last several trips; you choose to display some of them and store the rest.
Your record collection spans many shelves and is covered with dust; you hardly ever play them.	You sell/trash/donate those LPs and you buy a few "greatest hits" CDs or only download those songs you will play and enjoy.

If you're not constantly reducing what you're holding on to, you're not acknowledging the reality of an era that keeps throwing more at you at home and at work than you can respond to. You've got enough to deal with in your home in the present; who needs the clutter of the past along with it?

55 **Store Creatively When Space Is Sparse** Face it, you probably find that you'll never have all the space you need. As such, you'll need to improvise at work and at home. Consider a house that lacks a full or even partial basement but does have a tiny cellar that is only big enough to accommodate one person at a time. Organization techniques in this space will also serve you well.

- Ensure that the small cellar is easily accessible, whether from inside your home or from an exterior entrance.

- Install a light nearby on a switch. If this is not feasible, use a dependable flashlight or suitable substitute.
- Don't keep anything on the steps, as it will almost inevitably cause someone to trip and fall.
- If floor space is limited, use the walls. Securely fasten supplies, tools, and other suitable items to the wall.
- Keep the area clean. Such cellars often accumulate dust and dirt in a hurry.
- Don't let your cellar become home to friendly little critters that leave you presents in the corners of the room.

If you need more storage space, consider freestanding storage units, which are available in varying sizes from hardware and home center stores at a surprisingly affordable price. Storage units may come preassembled or in modular form that you can assemble on your own. However, they enable you to maintain a fine level of organization because you can store things in them that otherwise clutter your garage or other storage areas attached to your home.

As with the small cellar, or garage for that matter, keep the storage area clean; use wall space to maximum advantage, and allow yourself the ability to easily maneuver within the storage unit. You don't want to be bumping into or falling over things. And with all the sharp and heavy objects in a garage—that's very beneficial to your health!

Keep the center of the storage unit clear and arrange your possessions around the facility in a U-type configuration. This will provide you with access to everything and you won't have to reach over something to get to something else.

Don't fall into the trap of overloading, like too many people so often do with cellars or other storage facilities in and around their homes. It starts off harmless enough, and for the first few months or even years, everything seems orderly. But before you know it, these spaces are jam-packed with stuff. Suddenly, it seems as if you have inadequate storage space!

Ah, but do you? You haven't cleaned out your storage room in the longest time. Such places represent hazards to those who dare to venture in. Some of these storage areas are firetraps containing flammable materials. Others represent accidents waiting to happen—there may be tools with sharp points that might injure someone. Take control of these spaces now before anyone gets hurt. In such cases, a little organization goes a long, long way! Someday, you might even be able to store your car in the garage! Then one cold winter morning, your car will start easier, become warm sooner, and have no snow on the windshield. Your drive to work may actually be nicer. What a crazy idea. . . .

56 **Buy Gifts with a Game Plan** Whether in your professional or personal life, it's difficult to buy presents for some people (and you know who they are!). Instead of feeling flustered the next time the look on a recipient's face betrays his or her true feelings about the gift, rethink how you shop. Adjusting how and when you shop can make buying less stressful for you. Moreover, you'll be more likely to buy a gift that's appreciated and that doesn't drain your bank account.

One of the most difficult chores at holiday time is finding the right gift for friends and family, and coworkers and colleagues (aside from battling never-ending lines and badgering employees dressed as elves, if you decide to brave the malls). Thankfully some people are easy to buy for, but there are those who are picky and those you don't know so well. Then, of course, there's always that one person on your list who wants for nothing—or at least tells you as much—but his story is quick to change if you fail to buy him a gift. Create a year-round holiday gift list to ease the burden of shopping. When a friend comments on something he or she likes, make note of it.

As you've discovered, everything and anything is available online, and with so many ways to find a good deal, why leave the sanctity of your PC? Legions of shopping sites like *www.nextag .com*, *www.pricegrabber.com*, *www.mysimon.com*, *www.dealtime .com*, and others are ready to assist you, if haven't already visited most of them! Some sites, such as *www.comparisonshopping.com*, even assess and compare shopping sites!

Still, there's something about being able to eyeball, touch, and fiddle around with a potential purchase, and you can't do that using the Web . . . yet. If you prefer to be out and about, carefully pick the days you shop. Mondays and Tuesdays are much less crowded than the weekends. No sense battling giggling middle-school girls or teenagers with painful-looking facial piercings if you don't have to.

If you work away from home, you may have to shop in the evenings. Since you'll be tired after your hectic workday, buy smaller gifts such as DVDs, CDs, gift certificates, and jewelry so you're not stuck carrying around large packages. Also, have the presents wrapped right in the store. Paying an extra dollar or two will save you the headache of wrapping at home—and keep you from making another mess to clean up.

If you're a stickler for doing things yourself, decorative bags are an easy (and attractive) way of wrapping gifts. Gift bags can be expensive, but many discount retailers and dollar stores offer inexpensive lines of gift bags, tissue paper, and accessories. Keep all the bags you receive so that you can reuse them. Just make sure there are no personal messages attached before you reuse them. Otherwise things could get awkward.

Invariably, there's someone you'll forget to shop for until the last minute. When this happens, go with the trusty gift certificate. Some malls offer mall-wide gift certificates that allow the recipient to choose a present at whichever store he or she prefers. Many people buy a few extra gifts in case they receive an unexpected gift from someone for whom they haven't purchased anything, like a neighbor or coworker. Buying one or two extra gifts is fine, but any more than that is excessive.

If some friends have a special hobby, buy a gift certificate from the store that caters to such hobbies. Or if they're a music lover, purchase an iTunes gift card so that they can download their favorite songs. Then when they listen to that song on their iPod, they'll think of you! Keep in mind that some people feel more loved when thought is put toward their gift and consider gift certificates a quick fix. Others are ecstatic that they can get what they actually want.

If you're in a pinch, to make it easy on yourself, order as many gifts as you can online or through the mail. As long as you order products a few weeks before you need them, there should be no problem with them arriving on time. However, be careful when you order. Ask for a specific delivery date and call the day before to confirm the package was sent. It would put a real damper on the holiday spirit if the presents didn't arrive in the mail until December 26. Ensure that you know correct sizes before you order to avoid sending everything back the next week.

While you're shopping for holiday gifts, pick up a few extra items for friends and family who have birthdays only a few months away. Although you may not want to contemplate any more holidays, you won't have to go shopping a month after Christmas. Once you get all your gifts home, keep all tags and receipts in one place where they are easy to find in case you need to take a gift back.

Most stores hold great sales on holiday items a few days after the holiday. This is a good time to buy wrapping paper, greeting cards, bows, boxes, and the like. It's also an opportunity to stock up on holiday craft and art supplies. You'll have everything you need when you start on next year's ornaments, decorations, and lights for your house. It's the most wonderful time of the year!

57 Systemize Your Shopping Much of what you buy comes with lengthy instruction manuals, warranty cards to be completed and mailed, and papers to file. At work or at home, how can you make optimal use of your purchases, master complex features, file the appropriate papers and packaging, and otherwise stay organized?

Prior to ever stepping foot in a store or ordering something online, determine what you actually want the product to be able to do. If you wait until you are on the showroom floor to ascertain the functions and features that you seek in an appliance or gadget, it's usually too late to enable you to make an optimal purchase and at a good price!

Develop a checklist of associated benefits and features of products that are attractive to you. I use a purchasing checklist to help ensure that I am getting the best deal before I spend money on something. After all, money doesn't grow on trees, you know. The following list discusses potential benefits and options related to stores or services responsible for selling the products you buy:

Discounts
- Are there quantity discounts or special terms?
- Are there corporate, government, association, or educator's discounts?
- Do they give weekly, monthly, or seasonal discounts?

- Do they offer frequent buyer discounts?
- Do they give off-peak discounts or odd-lot discounts?
- Do they offer a guaranteed lowest price?

Ordering Options
- Do they accept major credit cards or debit cards?
- Do they accept orders by fax or by e-mail?
- Do they offer a money-back guarantee or other guarantees?
- Do they have a toll-free ordering line and a customer service line?
- Is it easy to reach a live operator?
- Can you order online instead of going into the store?

Delivery
- Do they guarantee the shipping date? How do they ship?
- Do they offer free delivery and installation?
- Are their shipments insured?
- Are there shipping and handling charges?
- How long for delivery?
- What else is included?

Privacy
- At your request, will they keep your name off their mailing list?
- Do they intend to sell, rent, or transfer your purchase information to others?

Other Considerations
- How long have they been in business?
- Are authorized dealer/repair services in your area?
- Does the product come with a warranty?

Once on site, I am focused and ready with a single, slim piece of paper in my hand. Most consumers don't take any such steps to organize before a purchase because it seems like too much work. For me, it is less work to ensure that I acquire the right appliance, model, make, and capabilities than to discover too late that a purchase doesn't provide what I sought from the beginning. A guy's got to have his standards, after all.

When you're on site in a store, you want to give the appliance a good workout. With the salesperson standing by, run through the sequence of steps as if you had already purchased the machine. Ensure that you understand how the darn thing works; don't wait until you're at home, on your own, alone, without guidance. Have the instructions explained to you repeatedly until you can't possibly fail. This is not the time to be macho; it's okay to ask for help. I won't tell anybody.

The salesperson is present to serve you, the consumer, not the other way around. Arrive with the mindset that you are there to gather information, not necessarily to buy.

If you can't understand how to operate the unit and run through its basic functions while you are in the store, then perhaps the fault lies not with you, not with the salesperson, but with the manufacturer. Consider clothes dryers, microwave units, blenders, and combination radio and alarm clocks and how some of them, mysteriously, seem to have instructions that are too ponderous to fathom, while others seem easy to operate.

Avoid thick instruction manuals. When contemplating an appliance purchase, do you ask to see accompanying manuals? Some manufacturers think it is impressive to strap you with a 180-page instruction book with tiny print. Who wants to read that?

As you peruse the packet of papers that comes with your appliance, including the instruction manual, diagram or schematic, and the warranty card, stay on the lookout for the at-a-glance instructions. These are condensed onto a single page or card, often laminated, mercifully listing the five, eight, ten, or twelve basic functions that 98 percent of buyers regularly use. If this card is illustrated or uses symbols or icons, all the better. You shouldn't have to teach yourself gobbledygook to figure out how to run the rinse cycle.

Taking the card in hand, see how easily you can operate the showroom model. Perhaps you need help from the salesperson at this juncture. That is okay; run through the card once with help, then a second time without it. If you can master what is on the card, then you've likely got it made in the shade.

Ideally, on the second run-through without help, you should be fairly adept at making the appliance operate using the simple instructions. If not, maybe there is a make and model on the next shelf that is even easier to operate and still performs the basic functions that you're seeking, but without the Geiger counter and nuclear pulse propulsion features. If you can't pronounce the name of the feature, chances are you don't need it.

To stay organized following the purchase of any appliances, equipment, or technological gadgets, file the receipt, diagrams or schematics, and any other associated paperwork as you normally would with a purchase, but keep the instruction manual and the at-a-glance instructions near the appliance itself. This works particularly well for DVD players or televisions since, in many cases, you can simply place the instructions under the unit.

Recognize that fewer switches, buttons, or dials may not mean that a product is less sophisticated or offers fewer benefits or features. Indeed, the opposite may be true. Only seek products and instructions designed with intelligence and with the consumer in mind.

58 **Stay on Top of Your Taxes, Without the Stress** Keeping accurate, complete tax information is a must in the life of the organized individual or family. If you take simple steps to ensure that you have the documentation necessary to back up your tax returns, you don't have to fret about the IRS on that fateful day when you might get called in for an audit.

Any office supply store today sells a variety of notebooks, binders, folders, dividers, and other office supplies that enable you to quickly and easily house the various documents, receipts, and vouchers related to both your income and your expenses, in addition to offering super-duper tax preparation software packages (more on this shortly). Some people maintain all of their deductible tax receipts in a folder with a compartment for each month of the year. Other, more involved folders allow you to file receipts on a weekly basis over the course of fifty-two weeks.

Personally, I find that a three-ring binder works as well as anything. You can insert dividers for each month, and add three-hole punched plastic sleeves that enable you to both store and view the receipts and documentation you accumulate. If your expenditures in any given month are considerable, simply use more than one sheet for that month. If that is unfathomable, you might want to reconsider some of your more frivolous purchases so that next month you have fewer receipts to file.

If you own property, you can make room within your binder specifically to record and house transactions related to such ownership. The same is true for other types of tax-related issues, such as expenditures for child care, employee business expenses, job search information, and depreciable assets.

A decent guide for how to set up your tax binder often comes from reviewing tax returns from previous years. Notice what kinds of tax forms you were required to file. You'll likely need room in your binder for that particular tax-related concern for the coming year as well. Some people use financial management software to record all income and expenses immediately after every transaction throughout the year. This is fine if you can maintain that kind of diligence, but it's not entirely necessary to use such programs to stay organized and effectively complete your taxes on time.

For most people, the majority of expenditures can readily be traced through the family checkbook and major credit cards. Increasingly, credit card vendors, such as Visa, MasterCard, American Express, and Discover issue a convenient, concise compendium by category of all expenditures you have made in the past year.

Obviously, if you make any cash expenditures that may be tax-deductible, you need to get a receipt. This could include cash donations to charitable organizations or any other out-of-pocket disbursements. To keep things easy for yourself, establish the practice of paying by credit or debit card for everything that could remotely be judged deductible on your tax return. That way, you will have complete documentation at the end of the year between these two major sources of financial information.

Pick a day, and take the receipts and documents and begin allocating them into like areas such as "airfare," "hotels," "work supplies," "school supplies," "utility bills," "new shoes," and "auto maintenance and repair." You already know these categories, as you have been dealing with them for years!

You may end up with fifteen or twenty piles on the table before you. May you have a sufficiently large table! Completely allocate the entire stack until every single shred of paper is filed someplace. For those items that are difficult to classify, create a file called "miscellaneous." Then paper clip, staple, or fasten them together in some other way so that you have fifteen or twenty reasonably neat piles.

Derive the sum for each category with a calculator, then write that sum on a sticky note attached to the first receipt. Then create a summary page of all the categories and all of the totals.

Carefully review the itemized statement from your major credit card company and include any expenses that appeared on their concise roster that weren't otherwise in your year-long file folder. Afterward, do the same with your checkbook.

If you wrote a check for an item that is deductible, but you have no other documentation for it, add that sum to the appropriate category. When you're done, you will have all the expense information you need to make complete and accurate claims on your tax returns, or at least enough documentation to survive an audit without too much trauma.

About Your Income

Proceed in the same way with wage or earning statements. Continue categorizing, fastening, and summing until you produce a single sheet that encapsulates your yearly income. This provides you with clear, complete documentation with which to file your taxes (it's hard to be funny when you're dealing with taxes.)

If you have received any notices from the IRS or your state's department of taxation in previous years, reread the notices, especially if they involved a correction to your statement. In that way, you can minimize the chance of making the same error for the current year's statement.

Tax Preparation Software

Tax preparation software works like a dream! If you are already using such software, then you know how much faster and easier it is to prepare your taxes than it was in the days when you had to tediously proceed line by line through each of the tax forms you were obligated to file. If you haven't used tax preparation software before, start now, or face another fifteen hours of complete and utter drudgery.

There are several vendors of tax preparation software such as H&R Block TaxCut (*www.taxcut.com*), Intuit's TurboTax (*www.turbotax.intuit.com*), TaxACT (*www.taxact.com*), and CompleteTax (*www.completetax.com*), among others. Virtually all vendors offer downloadable versions of the software. You can even visit the Tax and Accounting Site Directory at *www.taxsites.com/software.html* to see a convenient compendium of tax preparation software for individuals, professionals, and companies.

In general, tax preparation software will save you hours of time and frustration in completing your tax returns. The variation among software programs is not prodigious. Each program has a user-friendly interface. You start off listing basic information; then, as you answer one question after another, the software assembles your information for appropriate and highly accurate use throughout your tax returns.

Based on the answers to the questions you provide, you proceed down one trail or down another. The software is designed so that you automatically file the forms that you need to complete based on your tax situation. Each of the software programs contains options that allow you to return to a prior screen, change data or information, prepare a tax worksheet on the fly, or examine actual return information.

Tax preparation software also allows you to pose "what if" questions. In other words, if you elect to file one way versus another, you can quickly see the ramifications of your selection. You can make April 15 the best day of the year! Okay, I exaggerated: You can make April 15 or whatever day you actually file a not-so-horrible day.

Handling State Income Taxes

In nearly every state in the union you also have to file state income taxes. These forms are somewhat less rigorous than IRS paperwork. Completing your state income taxes takes but a fraction of the time that is required to file your federal income taxes. Again, use your returns from prior years to serve as reasonable guides as to how to complete your current year's state return.

How does one get started on state taxes? I suggest buying the state versions of tax preparation software. Many of the vendors will give you a discount off the state version if you have already bought their federal version. When you use state tax preparation software, your overall transaction time is greatly reduced, often to ten minutes or less. You have the satisfaction of knowing that there is a decent probability that all the right forms have been filled out correctly. Your printer spits them out in rapid fashion, and as with the federal forms, they come to you neat, complete, and ready to be mailed.

If you send in your returns before March 15, you'll probably receive a refund in a few weeks. After April 1, you are competing with the masses who have procrastinated. As April 15 approaches, you are one of many taxpayers nationwide who are racing to get their forms turned in on time.

This may seem funny (as in odd) in a book on organization, but seek to help the IRS as much as you can. At the IRS, basically one person reviews your tax returns. Any explanations you can offer above and beyond the minuscule amount of space provided on the form can prove helpful. Moreover, it shows the IRS agent that you are a conscientious citizen and taxpayer, and that you are trying to be helpful. This can only work in your favor, especially if the agent who receives your information is particularly grumpy. Take it on faith, you don't want to make the IRS angry!

List the phone numbers where you can be reached and even your e-mail address. Any agent can find this information about you with ease, so you might as well provide it up front.

59 **Seek an Organizing Specialist** Got help? Have you considered the services of a professional organizer? They do exist, and they can be of significant assistance. Professional organizers will charge you at least $60 per hour. The good ones help you to not only get organized, but to stay organized as well. Together, you examine the areas of your work and life that have become disorganized and rearrange them so that they work for you.

A good professional organizer stresses principles, not merely placement. If you have an organizer arrive and simply "do everything for you" without teaching principles and without making you take an active role in the process, you're not likely to maintain any of your places and spaces. Sure enough, in a matter of time, things will become disorganized again.

When you know the reason for putting pens to the right, fins to the left (for all you Jimmy Buffet fans), paper in the top center drawer, and so on, you have a better chance of maintaining your system. After the professional organizer departs, do you want to be a long-term dependent? I mean, come on, do you want to have to pay somebody a pretty penny or voluminous stacks of $20 bills every time your stuff gets out of control? I think not!

If you think it makes sense to have a professional organizer help you for some finite number of sessions, or on a regular basis, then your best bet is to contact the National Association of Professional Organizers at *www.napo.net* to help you identify members in your local area. If you read and actually follow the tips in this book, however, you'll have no need to pay good money for a professional organizer. You've been cured!

60 **Divide, Literally, and Conquer** Now timeless wisdom in the form of a parting fable. When I was fourteen years old, my mother suggested that I reorganize our utility closet. Even at that age, I realized that this little room would never stay organized unless I had some way to divide and permanently separate items. The room was about 5 by 5 feet with no door; it had an entrance downstairs next to the laundry room. As you entered, to the right there were five built-in shelves; to the left there were clothing hooks hung in a single row for coats and jackets. Although it was a small room, it seemed to be a mess beyond reason and hope. The room served as our household catchall and contained tennis balls, wires, excess telephone cords, gloves, mittens, nuts and bolts, flashlights, batteries, and some objects whose identities I couldn't figure out for the life of me!

I hunted throughout the house to find empty shoeboxes and was able to gather about six or seven, which seemed like enough. I returned to the utility closet and began grouping like items together. I started with the middle shelf because it was the easiest to see and reach. There were enough stray tennis balls, racket balls, Ping-Pong balls, and golf balls to fit in one large shoebox. Then I used another shoebox to house wires, phone cords, extensions, extra light switches, wall outlets, and other small electrical stuff.

Since I didn't have all the shoeboxes I needed, I placed mittens, gloves, and scarves neatly in between the "ball" box and the "electrical" box. Using another shoebox, I housed extra doorstops, furniture savers (small, circular rubber mats that go under table legs and couches to preserve the rugs), dusting items, a whisk broom, and other stuff that didn't seem to fit anyplace else.

In the next space, I assembled cans and canisters that would remain upright and in place, such as insect spray, all-purpose oil, poison ivy lotion, plant food sprayers, and other such items. Once again, I did not use a shoebox; instead, I let the borders between shoeboxes serve as a compartment. Now the entire shelf, which consisted of five compartments, was complete. The shelf was visually pleasing and much more organized than before I had started. I was amazed I could actually see the shelf! I went on to tackle the other shelves in the same manner and spirit.

In the space between the floor and the bottom of the first shelf, I placed the largest items—those which, if they were to fall, would cause a ruckus. On higher shelves, I placed the lightest items, those seldom used, and perhaps most important, those that could easily be seen by a shorter person such as my mother.

Some of the items I encountered didn't belong in this utility closet at all. No surprise about that. I relocated such items to their proper homes in the garage, the laundry room, the kitchen, or the back deck. Some items didn't merit retention, so I went ahead and threw them away. Some items were unnecessary duplicates, so I gave them away.

When the project was complete, I stood back and examined the results. The closet that had been a total mess was now neat, functional, and (dare I say it?) roomy! The actual time to rearrange each shelf was no more than a few minutes. Reallocating items that were best suited to other locations throughout the house took several more minutes, but this was not a difficult task, and my fondness for organization was henceforth sealed!

A few years later when I was a senior in high school and then a college student, my organizational efforts in this particular room continued to prevail—no lie! Literally dividing up the items and creating permanent separations was the key. Sure, a couple of items were out of place, and the compartments on each shelf weren't quite so neat. Also, some new items had been put in the closet, presumably for me to come by and integrate!

Six years after my initial efforts, even in the face of the entropy that transpires in a household of six people and a cat, the utility closet remained organized. My organizational artistry had prevailed, and the insights I gained stayed with me through the decades.

At work, at home, and everywhere in between, if you have the containers, dividers, and tools, the physical organization of a space or place in your life is manageable. You can win. You can keep your possessions in order. You can find them when you need them. You can then show off your marvelous work. You can get organized!

Summary

With each passing year, and more specifically, each day, hour, minute, and second, an increasing amount of information is generated on earth and an accelerating number of technological breakthroughs are achieved. So maintaining organization in your career as well as in your personal life will only grow in importance while being more of a challenge.

Fortunately, you have the skills, the smarts, and the fortitude to stay in control. Even if you have an ultra-demanding job and considerable professional and personal responsibilities, you can succeed magnificently. When you acknowledge that you steer the rudder, flip the switch, pull the lever, call the shots, and have the power within you to take steps to make your life more organized, something wonderful occurs—your life starts to become more organized. If you've resolved to get organized, then you're well on the road to this achievement. Nothing can stop you.

Bibliography

Archibald, Russell, D. *Managing High-Technology Programs and Projects*. New York: Wiley, 1998.

Aslett, Don. *Clutter Free Finally and Forever.* Pocatello, ID: Marsh Creek Press, 1995.

Cathcart, Jim. *The Acorn Principle*. New York: St. Martin's Press, 1998.

Culbertson, Judi. *The Clutter Cure*. New York: McGraw-Hill, 2007.

Davidson, Jeff. *Breathing Space*. Charleston, SC: Booksurge, 2007.

Davidson, Jeff. *The Complete Idiot's Guide to Getting Things Done*. New York: Alpha Books, 2005.

Davidson, Jeff. *The Complete Idiot's Guide to Managing Your Time*. New York: Alpha Books, 2002.

Davidson, Jeff. *The 60 Second Self-Starter*. Avon, MA: Adams Media, 2008.

Eisenberg, Ronni. *Organize Your Life: Free Yourself From Clutter and Find More Personal Time*. Hoboken, NJ: Wiley, 2007.

Felton, Sandra. *Messies Manual*. Grand Rapids, MI: Fleming Revel, 1983.

Fritz, Robert. *The Path of Least Resistance*. New York: Ballantine, 1989.

Hall, Edward. *The Hidden Dimension*. New York: Doubleday, 1966.

Hemphill, Barbara. *Taming the Paper Tiger*. Washington: Kiplinger Books, 1996.

Kostner, Jaclyn. *Knights for the TeleRound Table*. New York: Warner, 1994.

Levasseur, Robert. *Breakthrough Business Meetings*. Avon, MA: Adams Media, 1994.

Markham, Ursula. *The Elements of Visualization*. Rockport, MA: Element Books, 1989.

Maslow, Abraham. *Toward a Psychology of Being*. New York: Wiley, 1968.

Moore-Ede, Martin. *The Twenty-Four-Hour Society*. Reading, MA: Addison-Wesley, 1993.

Moskowitz, Robert. *How to Organize Your Work and Your Life*. San Diego: Mainstream Books, 1981.

Pagonis, William. *Moving Mountains.* Cambridge, MA: Harvard Business School Press, 1992.

Salsbury, Glenna. *The Art of the Fresh Start*. Deerfield Beach, FL: Health Communications, 1995.

Stack, Laura. *Find More Time: How to Get Things Done at Home, Organize Your Life, and Feel Great About It*. New York: Broadway Books, 2006.

Sugarman, Joseph. *Success Forces*. Chicago: Contemporary Books, 1980.

Zeer, Darrin. *Office Yoga: Simple Stretches for Busy People*. San Francisco: Chronicle Books, 2000.

About the Author

JEFF DAVIDSON knows a thing or two about getting organized, and how to enhance one's professional and personal life as a result. He is among the best at offering solutions to the time pressures and life balance problems that people face today—people like you! Jeff mixes "tried and true" advice with fresh insights and innovative solutions to the daily career and personal problems that often confront people.

Jeff has been featured in seventy-two of the top seventy-five newspapers in America, based on circulation, including *USA Today,* the *New York Times,* the *Washington Post,* the *Los Angeles Times,* the *Christian Science Monitor*, and the *Chicago Tribune*. As a five-time state winner of the United States Small Business Administration's Media Advocate of the Year Award, Jeff has published more than 3,550 articles on the topics of life balance, management and marketing effectiveness, and career advancement in nearly every type of magazine, journal, newsletter, and online posting.

Jeff's speeches have been featured in Vital Speeches of the Day on eight occasions along with people including Alan Greenspan, Dr. Henry Kissinger, Lee Iacocca, George H. W. Bush, William Bennett, Michael Eisner, Jimmy Carter, and the Dalai Lama. He has shared the spotlight on covers of magazines with Tony Robbins and with Dr. Wayne Dyer.

For six years running, Jeff has averaged 100,000 books sold annually in the highly competitive fields of self-help, business, and how-to books. Some of his titles include *The 60 Second Self-Starter, The Complete Guide to Public Speaking, Breathing Space,* and *The Complete Idiot's Guide to Time Management*, along with six other titles in that series.

As a professional speaker, Jeff has attracted clients such as American Express, America Online, Cardinal Health Systems, Dollar Rent-a-Car, Dunhill Staffing, Executone, IBM, Lufthansa, NationsBank, Re/Max, SFX Sports Group, Swisshotel, Syngenta, Vanguard Managed Solutions, Wells Fargo, Westinghouse, Worthington Steel, and more than 700 other leading organizations and associations including the U.S. Treasury, American Bankers Association, National Association of Realtors, Club Managers Association of America, and the American Congress of Healthcare Executives.

Jeff can be reached via e-mail at *Jeff@BreathingSpace.com* and found on the Web at *www.BreathingSpace.com,* which offers information on his keynote speeches and seminars, including "No Time, No Clarity? No Problem!"™ "Managing the Pace with Grace,"® "Choosing When It's Confusing,"® and "Managing Information and Communication Overload."®